Cookies

A collection of 200 delicious recipes

Contents

Introduction

The cookies included in this book are easy and enjoyable to make, fun to eat and great to share whatever the time of day. Every home should have a well-stocked jar of them waiting to be dipped into, and they are the perfect choice for a mid-morning coffee or afternoon tea, at a children's party or on a festive occasion. Whatever the reason, you are sure to find what you are looking for among the 200 delicious goodies that have been gathered together in this collection.

The making of cookies started in ancient Egypt with a mixture of flour and water that was baked on both sides on a griddle, resulting in a flat, hard cake. To this mixture, leaveners were added to make the cake rise, and then sugar to sweeten it. Wood-burning and coal-fired ovens were developed, and from these humble beginnings, cookies have evolved. Today every country has its own favourite recipe, be it chocolate chip cookies, biscotti or oatcakes – the list is endless!

The star ingredients

Sugar, fat, eggs, flour and a liquid are the basic ingredients that the majority of the recipes share.

Sugar
Caster sugar is usually recommended because it dissolves more easily than granulated sugar. Nevertheless, granulated sugar can be used if necessary.

Fat
Butter is the fat that is suggested in most of the recipes, as this adds richness and gives the best flavour. However, margarine can be used as an alternative, and is less expensive. It is important, though, to use a margarine containing not less that 60 per cent fat; choose a hard margarine that is described on the packet as suitable for baking. The exception is when a recipe calls for a soft margarine. In this instance all the ingredients are beaten together with an electric whisk until mixed.

Eggs
The size of eggs used in the recipes is medium unless otherwise stated. If possible, use eggs that are at room temperature because cold eggs can cause the mixture to curdle and will result in a less soft mixture.

Flour
The flour used in the recipes may be plain or self-raising. Should you need self-raising flour but only have plain, sift 2½ teaspoons of baking powder into every 225 g/ 8 oz plain flour.

Liquid
The liquid in the recipes is used to bind the ingredients together and is usually milk, eggs, butter, oil, water or fruit juice.

Assuring success

Almost all the recipes in the book are easy to make. Follow these useful suggestions and you will be guaranteed success every time:

• Preheat the oven for 10–15 minutes before baking, even if the oven manufacturer's instructions suggest that this is not necessary. If you have a fan-assisted oven, reduce the temperature according to their instructions.

• It is important that ingredients are measured accurately, so it is worth investing in good-quality scales and standard measuring spoons.

• Get into the habit of preparing baking sheets and tins before commencing preparation, as mixtures that contain self-raising flour start to activate once the liquid has been added to them and should therefore be baked as soon as possible after they have been prepared.

• When butter or hard margarine needs to be softened before blending with another ingredient, either remove it from the refrigerator and leave at room temperature for about 1 hour, or cut into cubes, place in a bowl and microwave on High for 10 seconds until softened slightly. Be careful not to allow it to melt.

• It is not necessary to sift flour unless you are combining several dry ingredients to facilitate even mixing.

• Where dough has to be refrigerated to make it firmer and easier to handle, you can speed this up by wrapping the dough in baking paper and placing in the freezer for a third of the time that you would normally refrigerate it.

• Do not over-beat bar cookie mixtures as this can make them rise too much and sink when they cool.

• Always place cookie dough on cold baking sheets to prevent the dough from spreading excessively and browning too much around the edges. When making a large quantity of cookies, leave the baking sheet to cool for a few minutes in between batches.

• Bake cookies on non-stick baking sheets or line them with baking paper but, unless specified in the recipe, do not grease the sheets as the cookies will spread excessively, become too thin and brown too quickly around the edges.

• Place cookies well apart on the baking sheet to allow room for them to spread during cooking. Unless they are particularly large, a gap of 5 cm/2 inches is usually enough.

• Position baking sheets on the middle rack of the oven for even browning.

• Unless otherwise stated, transfer cookies to a wire rack as soon as they are firm enough to handle and leave to cool. This will allow the steam to evaporate and prevent them from becoming soggy.

Equipment & helpful techniques

To make any of the recipes in this book requires very little special equipment and, in many cases, improvisation can be helpful! Nevertheless, here are some suggestions that you may find useful:

● Use your hands! Dampen them slightly when shaping cookies into a ball.

● A hand-held electric whisk is useful for whisking and beating mixtures together but, failing this, use a balloon whisk for whisking and a wooden spoon for creaming.

● When making bar cookies, recipes that specify a particular size of tin can equally be made in a tin with different dimensions but the same capacity.

● Use a food processor for rubbing fat into flour, but when the eggs or liquid are added make sure you blend them quickly, as overworked dough will be tough.

● When preparing a tin for baking bar cookies, especially one that is not shallow, line with baking paper, letting it hang over the edge of the tin. This makes it easier when lifting and removing the cookies later.

● If a recipe asks for toasted nuts and you do not have any, you can toast them yourself. Preheat the oven to 180°C/350°F/ Gas Mark 4. Spread the nuts in a single layer on a baking sheet and cook in the preheated oven for 5–10 minutes, turning and watching them carefully until golden brown.

To melt chocolate

Many of the recipes require you to melt chocolate in a heatproof bowl set over a saucepan of simmering water. This is the safest way to melt it because it will not overheat and become dry. Make sure the bowl does not touch the water.

Bake & store

With a few exceptions, most of the cookies in this book will keep well in a tin or airtight container and, in the case of bar cookies, even in the baking tin in which they were cooked, if it is kept tightly covered with foil. The following tips will also help, however:

● Ideally, store baked cookies undecorated. Any item that is decorated with dairy products should be stored in the refrigerator.

● Store soft cookies separately from crisp varieties so that they don't all become soft.

● Store different flavoured cookies separately so that their flavours do not mingle together.

● Only store cookies when they are completely cold because if stored while still warm they are liable to stick together.

● One or two sugar cubes added to a tin of cookies helps to keep them crisp.

● Most cookies can be frozen and thawed at short notice, but most are best when just baked.

The presentation

Finally, when serving your cookies, remember presentation makes all the difference. Serve the delicate types on fine china or glass plates, or use cake stands and baskets lined with napkins, or even tins lined with baking paper.

The beautifully photographed recipes in this book will capture your imagination – and with 200 of them to choose from you are really spoilt for choice!

1 Chocolate chip cookies

115 g/4 oz butter, softened, plus extra
    for greasing
115 g/4 oz light muscovado sugar
1 egg
100 g/3½ oz porridge oats
1 tbsp milk
1 tsp vanilla extract

125 g/4½ oz plain flour
1 tbsp cocoa powder
½ tsp baking powder
175 g/6 oz plain chocolate, broken
    into pieces
175 g/6 oz milk chocolate, broken
    into pieces

Preheat the oven to 180°C/350°F/Gas Mark 4. Grease 2 large baking sheets. Place the butter and sugar in a large bowl and beat together until light and fluffy. Beat in the egg, then add the oats, milk and vanilla extract and beat together until well blended. Sift the flour, cocoa and baking powder into the mixture and stir. Stir in the chocolate pieces.

Place dessertspoonfuls of the mixture on the baking sheets and flatten slightly with a fork. Bake in the preheated oven for 15 minutes, or until slightly risen and firm.

Leave to cool on the baking sheets for 2 minutes, then transfer the cookies to wire racks to cool completely.

2 White chocolate chip cookies

Replace the plain and milk chocolate with 275 g/9¾ oz chopped white chocolate.

3 Almond cookies with a cherry on top

200 g/7 oz butter, cut into cubes, plus
    extra for greasing
90 g/3¼ oz caster sugar
½ tsp almond extract

280 g/10 oz self-raising flour
25 g/1 oz ground almonds
25 glacé cherries (total weight about
    125 g/4½ oz)

Preheat the oven to 180°C/350°F/Gas Mark 4. Grease several large baking sheets.

Place the butter in a large saucepan and heat gently until melted. Remove from the heat. Add the sugar and almond extract to the pan and stir together. Add the flour and ground almonds and mix to form a smooth dough.

Roll small pieces of the dough between your hands into smooth balls to make 25 in total. Place on the baking sheets, spaced well apart, and flatten slightly with your hands, then press a cherry gently into the centre of each cookie. Bake in the preheated oven for 10–15 minutes, or until golden brown.

Leave to cool for 2–3 minutes on the baking sheets, then transfer the cookies to a wire rack to cool completely.

4 Cookies & cream sandwiches

125 g/4½ oz butter, softened
75 g/2¾ oz icing sugar
115 g/4 oz plain flour
40 g/1½ oz cocoa powder
½ tsp ground cinnamon

FILLING
125 g/4½ oz plain chocolate, broken
   into pieces
50 ml/2 fl oz double cream

Preheat the oven to 160°C/325°F/Gas Mark 3. Line 2 large baking sheets with baking paper. Place the butter and sugar in a large bowl and beat together until light and fluffy. Sift the flour, cocoa and cinnamon into the mixture and mix to form a dough.

Place the dough between 2 sheets of baking paper and roll out until the dough is 3 mm/⅛ inch thick. Cut out 6-cm/2½-inch rounds and place on the baking sheets. Bake in the preheated oven for 15 minutes, or until firm to the touch. Leave to cool for 2 minutes on the baking paper, then transfer the cookies to wire racks to cool completely.

Meanwhile, make the filling. Place the chocolate and cream in a saucepan and heat gently until the chocolate has melted. Stir until smooth. Leave to cool, then chill in the refrigerator for 2 hours, or until firm. Sandwich the biscuits together in pairs with a spoonful of the chocolate cream and serve.

5 With strawberry filling

Replace the plain chocolate with white chocolate, chop 85 g/3 oz dried strawberries into small pieces and fold into the chilled filling.

6 Classic oatmeal biscuits

175 g/6 oz butter or margarine, plus
   extra for greasing
275 g/9¾ oz demerara sugar
1 egg
4 tbsp water

1 tsp vanilla extract
375 g/13 oz rolled oats
140 g/5 oz plain flour
1 tsp salt
½ tsp bicarbonate of soda

Preheat the oven to 180°C/350°F/Gas Mark 4. Grease 2 large baking sheets. Place the butter and sugar in a large bowl and beat together until light and fluffy. Beat in the egg, water and vanilla extract until the mixture is smooth. Mix the oats, flour, salt and bicarbonate of soda together in a separate bowl, then gradually stir the oat mixture into the creamed mixture until thoroughly combined.

Place tablespoonfuls of the mixture onto the baking sheets, spaced well apart. Bake in the preheated oven for 15 minutes, or until golden brown. Transfer to a wire rack to cool completely.

7 Oatmeal & vine fruit biscuits

Add 85 g/3 oz chopped sultanas and raisins to the dough mix.

8 Chocolate sprinkle cookies

MAKES 30

225 g/8 oz butter, softened
140 g/5 oz caster sugar
1 egg yolk, lightly beaten
2 tsp vanilla extract
225 g/8 oz plain flour, plus extra
   for dusting

55 g/2 oz cocoa powder
pinch of salt
200 g/7 oz white chocolate, broken
   into pieces
85 g/3 oz chocolate vermicelli

Place the butter and sugar in a large bowl and mix well with a wooden spoon, then beat in the egg yolk and vanilla extract.

Sift together the flour, cocoa and salt into the mixture and stir until thoroughly combined. Halve the dough, roll each piece into a ball, wrap in clingfilm and chill in the refrigerator for 30–60 minutes.

Preheat the oven to 190°C/ 375°F/Gas Mark 5. Line 2 large baking sheets with baking paper.

Unwrap the dough and roll out between 2 pieces of baking paper to about 5 mm/¼ inch thick. Cut out 30 cookies with a 6–7-cm/2½–2¾-inch fluted round cutter and place them on the baking sheets, spaced well apart. Bake in the preheated oven for 10–12 minutes. Leave to cool on the baking sheets for 5–10 minutes, then transfer the cookies to wire racks to cool completely.

Place the white chocolate in a heatproof bowl, set the bowl over a saucepan of gently simmering water and heat until melted. Immediately remove from the heat and spread the melted chocolate over the cookies. Leave to cool slightly then sprinkle with the chocolate vermicelli. Leave to cool and set before serving.

9 Marbled cookies

Omit the chocolate vermicelli and use 100 g/3½ oz melted plain chocolate to swirl into the white chocolate topping to create a marbled effect.

10 Shortbread

MAKES 8

115 g/4 oz butter, cut into small pieces,
   plus extra for greasing
175 g/6 oz plain flour, plus extra
   for dusting

pinch of salt
55 g/2 oz caster sugar, plus extra
   for sprinkling

Preheat the oven to 150°C/300°F/Gas Mark 2. Grease a loose-bottomed 20-cm/8-inch round fluted tart tin with butter.

Place the flour, salt and sugar in a large bowl and mix together. Add the butter and rub it into the dry ingredients. Continue to work the mixture until it forms a soft dough. Make sure you do not overwork the shortbread or it will be tough.

Lightly press the dough into the tart tin. If you don't have a fluted tin, roll out the dough on a lightly floured board, place on a baking sheet and pinch the edges to form a scalloped pattern.

Using a knife, mark the dough into 8 pieces and prick all over with a fork. Bake in the preheated oven for 45–50 minutes, or until the shortbread is firm and just coloured. Leave to cool for a few minutes in the tin, then sprinkle with sugar. Cut into portions and transfer to a wire rack to cool.

11 Lemon & vanilla shortbread

Split a vanilla pod in half lengthways, carefully scrape out the seeds and add to the flour along with the finely grated rind of 1 lemon.

175 g/6 oz butter, softened
50 g/1¾ oz icing sugar, plus extra
    for dusting
1 small egg yolk

2½ tsp brandy
375 g/13 oz plain white flour
¼ tsp baking powder

Preheat the oven to 180°C/350°F/Gas Mark 4. Line 2–3 large baking sheets with baking paper.

Place the butter and icing sugar in a large bowl and beat together until light and fluffy. Add the egg yolk and brandy and beat until the mixture is smooth. Sift the flour and baking powder into the mixture and beat until combined then, using your hands, knead the mixture until smooth.

Roll small pieces of the dough into smooth balls, then place them on the baking sheets, spaced well apart, and flatten slightly with your hands. Bake in the preheated oven for 15 minutes, or until firm to the touch and pale golden brown. Meanwhile, sift a layer of icing sugar into a large roasting tin.

Leave the shortbread to cool for 2–3 minutes on the baking sheets, then place in the roasting tin in a single layer. Sift more icing sugar generously over the top and leave to cool completely.

13 Greek almond shortbread

Use only 2 teaspoons of brandy and add ½ teaspoon of almond extract. Replace 125 g/4½ oz of the flour with ground almonds.

14 Greek pistachio shortbread

Add 50 g/1¾ oz finely chopped pistachio nuts to the mixture after adding the flour and baking powder.

15 Greek lemon shortbread

Add the finely grated rind of 1 lemon to the mixture with the egg yolk and replace the brandy with 2½ teaspoons of lemon juice.

115 g/4 oz unsalted butter, softened
50 g/1¾ oz demerara sugar
1 large egg, separated
½ tsp vanilla extract
140 g/5 oz plain flour
pinch of salt
150 g/5½ oz chopped mixed nuts

36 chocolate- or sugar-coated peanuts,
   to decorate

ICING
225 g/8 oz butter, softened
1 tbsp cream or milk
350 g/12 oz icing sugar

Place the butter and sugar in a large bowl and beat together until light and fluffy. Stir in the egg yolk and vanilla extract and beat together, then add the flour and salt and beat to combine. Wrap the dough in clingfilm and chill in the refrigerator for 3 hours.

Preheat the oven to 180°C/350°F/Gas Mark 4. Line a large baking sheet with baking paper.

Lightly whisk the egg white in a clean bowl and spread the chopped nuts out on a plate. Roll walnut-sized pieces of the dough into balls. Dip each ball in the egg white then roll in the nuts to coat and place on the baking sheet. Bake in the preheated oven for 5 minutes, then remove and make an indentation with your thumb in the middle of each cookie. Bake for a further 5 minutes, then leave the cookies to cool completely on the baking sheet.

To make the buttercream icing, place the butter in a large bowl and beat until soft. Sift in the icing sugar and beat together until smooth. Spoon a little filling into the indentation of each cookie and top each one with 2 chocolate- or sugar-coated peanuts.

17 *With hazelnut & chocolate topping*

Replace the buttercream icing with 140 g/5 oz hazelnut chocolate spread.

175 g/6 oz unsalted butter, softened,
   plus extra for greasing
200 g/7 oz caster sugar
1 large egg, lightly beaten
1 tsp vanilla extract or almond extract
300 g/10½ oz plain flour, plus extra
   for dusting
pinch of salt

TOPPING
150 g/5½ oz icing sugar
about 1 tbsp cold water
yellow, pink and blue food colouring
silver dragées
coloured writing icing

Place the butter and sugar in a large bowl and beat together until light and fluffy. Whisk the egg and vanilla together in a separate bowl, then beat into the butter mixture. Sift in the flour and salt and mix to form a dough. Wrap in clingfilm and chill for 30 minutes.

Preheat the oven to 180°C/350°F/Gas Mark 4. Grease a large baking sheet. Roll the dough out on a floured work surface to 5 mm/¼ inch thick. Cut out shapes with a flour-dipped butterfly-shaped cookie cutter and place on the baking sheet. Bake in the preheated oven for 12–15 minutes, or until they are golden brown. Leave to cool on wire racks.

To make the icing, sift the icing sugar into a bowl, add the water and mix until smooth. Divide the icing into portions and tint to pastel shades with food colouring. Spread the icing over the cookies and decorate with silver dragées. Leave to set, then finish decorating with writing icing.

175 g/6 oz unsalted butter, softened
100 g/3½ oz soft light brown sugar
1 large egg, lightly beaten
1 tbsp clear honey
280 g/10 oz plain flour, plus extra
    for dusting
½ tsp ground cinnamon

TO DECORATE
115 g/4 oz icing sugar
about ½ tsp cold water
3 tbsp chocolate sprinkles
20 gum drops
coloured writing icing

Place the butter and sugar in a large bowl and beat together until
light and fluffy. Add the egg and honey and stir to combine. Sift in the
flour and cinnamon and mix to form a soft dough. Wrap the dough in
clingfilm and chill in the refrigerator for 30 minutes.

Preheat the oven to 190°C/375°F/Gas Mark 5. Line a large baking
sheet with baking paper. Cut the dough in half and roll in the remaining
flour, then roll out each piece between 2 sheets of clingfilm. Using a
7-cm/2¾-inch cookie cutter, cut out 10 discs from each piece and place
on the baking sheet. Bake in the preheated oven for 10–12 minutes,
or until golden brown. Leave to cool for 5 minutes, then transfer the
cookies to a wire rack to cool completely.

Sift the icing sugar into a bowl, add the water and mix until smooth.
Spread the cookies with a thin layer of icing, then use the chocolate
sprinkles for hair and a gum drop for the nose. Leave to set, then draw
in the eyes and mouth with the writing icing.

20 *Fairy faces*

*For fairy faces, ice the biscuits according to the recipe but use 3 tablespoons
of pink sprinkles for the hair and use pink writing icing for the face.*

21 *Buttery fork cookies*   MAKES 25

125 g/4½ oz unsalted butter, softened
125 g/4½ oz caster sugar
1 large egg yolk

100 g/3½ oz plain flour
1 tsp ground cinnamon

Preheat the oven to 200°C/400°F/Gas Mark 6. Line a large baking sheet
with baking paper.

Place the butter and 25 g/1 oz of the sugar in a large bowl and beat
together until light and fluffy. Add the egg yolk and mix together, then
sift in the flour and mix to form a soft dough.

Mix the remaining sugar with the cinnamon. Take a teaspoon of
dough and roll it in the sugar mixture. Place on the baking sheet and
use a fork to press down until the cookie is 1 cm/½ inch thick. Repeat
until all the dough is used up. Bake in the preheated oven for 10
minutes, or until golden brown. Leave to cool on a wire rack.

22 *Coconut buttery fork cookies*

*Add 100 g/3½ oz shredded coconut to the dough and roll the cookies in the
remaining caster sugar, but omit the cinnamon.*

23 *Christmas angels*

225 g/8 oz butter, softened
140 g/5 oz caster sugar
1 egg yolk, lightly beaten
2 tsp passion fruit pulp
280 g/10 oz plain flour
pinch of salt
55 g/2 oz desiccated coconut

TO DECORATE
175 g/6 oz icing sugar
1–1½ tbsp passion fruit pulp
edible silver glitter

Place the butter and sugar in a large bowl and beat together until light and fluffy then beat in the egg yolk and passion fruit pulp. Sift together the flour and salt into the mixture, add the coconut and stir until thoroughly combined. Halve the dough, shape into balls, wrap in clingfilm and chill for 30–60 minutes.

Preheat the oven to 190°C/375°F/Gas Mark 5. Line 2 baking sheets with baking paper.

Unwrap the dough and roll out between 2 sheets of baking paper. Cut out cookies with a 7-cm/2¾-inch angel-shaped cutter and place them on the baking sheets, spaced well apart.

Bake in the preheated oven for 10–15 minutes, or until light golden brown. Leave to cool for 5–10 minutes, then transfer to wire racks to cool completely.

Sift the icing sugar into a bowl and stir in the passion fruit pulp until it is the consistency of thick cream. Leave the cookies on the racks and spread the icing over them. Sprinkle with the edible glitter and leave to set.

24 *Angel ornaments*

Before baking, make a hole with a metal skewer or straw in the top of each cookie. Check the holes are big enough when the cookies come out of the oven and re-pierce if necessary. Cool and decorate as before. Using thin white ribbon, string chains of the angels together to hang on the Christmas tree.

25 *Christmas bells*

225 g/8 oz butter, softened
140 g/5 oz caster sugar
finely grated rind of 1 lemon
1 egg yolk, lightly beaten
280 g/10 oz plain flour
½ tsp ground cinnamon
pinch of salt
100 g/3½ oz plain chocolate chips

TO DECORATE
2 tbsp lightly beaten egg white
2 tbsp lemon juice
225 g/8 oz icing sugar
30 silver dragées
food colouring pens

Place the butter, sugar and lemon rind in a large bowl and beat together until light and fluffy, then beat in the egg yolk. Sift together the flour, cinnamon and salt into the mixture, add the chocolate chips and stir until thoroughly combined. Halve the dough, shape into balls, wrap in clingfilm and chill in the refrigerator for 30–60 minutes.

Preheat the oven to 190°C/375°F/Gas Mark 5. Line 2 large baking sheets with baking paper. Unwrap the dough and roll out between 2 sheets of baking paper. Cut out cookies with a 5-cm/2-inch bell-shaped cutter and place them on the baking sheets, spaced well apart.

Bake in a preheated oven for 10–15 minutes, or until light golden brown. Leave the cookies to cool for 5–10 minutes, then

transfer to wire racks to cool completely.

Mix the egg white and lemon juice together in a bowl, then gradually beat in the icing sugar until smooth. Leave the cookies on the racks and spread the icing over them. Place a silver dragée on the clapper shape at the bottom of the cookie and leave to set completely. When the icing is dry, use the food colouring pens to draw patterns on the cookies.

26 *Coloured bells*

Divide the icing into 3 portions. Leave one white, colour one portion with red food colouring and the third with green and use to decorate the bells. Leave to set, then tie 3 cookies together in a stack, one of each colour, using ribbon.

Christmas tree decorations

225 g/8 oz butter, softened
140 g/5 oz caster sugar
1 egg yolk, lightly beaten
2 tsp vanilla extract
280 g/10 oz plain flour
pinch of salt

1 egg white, lightly beaten
2 tbsp hundreds and thousands
400 g/14 oz fruit-flavoured boiled sweets
   in different colours
25 lengths of ribbon, to hang

Place the butter and sugar into a bowl and beat together until light and fluffy, then beat in the egg yolk and vanilla extract. Sift together the flour and salt into the mixture and stir until combined. Halve the dough, shape into balls, wrap in clingfilm and chill for 30–60 minutes.

Preheat the oven to 190°C/375°F/Gas Mark 5. Line 2 large baking sheets with baking paper. Unwrap the dough and roll out between 2 sheets of baking paper. Cut out cookies with Christmas-themed cutters and place them on the baking sheets, spaced well apart.

Using the end of a large plain piping nozzle, cut out rounds from each shape and remove them. Make a small hole in the top of each cookie with a skewer so that they can be threaded with ribbon. Brush with egg white and sprinkle with hundreds and thousands. Bake in the preheated oven for 7 minutes. Meanwhile, lightly crush the sweets by tapping them with a rolling pin. Unwrap and sort into separate bowls

by colour. Remove the cookies from the oven and fill the holes with the crushed sweets. Return to the oven and bake for a further 5–8 minutes, or until they are light golden brown and the sweets have melted and filled the holes. Leave to cool on the baking sheets and then transfer to wire racks. Thread thin ribbon through the holes in the top and hang.

Star-shaped cookies

75 g/6 oz plain flour, plus extra
   for dusting
1 tsp ground cinnamon
1 tsp ground ginger
90 g/3¼ oz butter, cut into cubes
85 g/3 oz soft light brown sugar
finely grated rind of 1 orange
1 egg, lightly beaten

TO DECORATE
200 g/7 oz icing sugar
3–4 tsp cold water
edible silver cake sparkles
silver dragées

Preheat the oven to 180°C/350°F/Gas Mark 4. Line several large baking sheets with baking paper.

Sift the flour, cinnamon and ginger into a large bowl. Add the butter and rub it in with your fingertips until the mixture

resembles fine breadcrumbs. Stir the sugar and orange rind into the mixture, add the egg and mix together to form a soft dough.

Roll the mixture out thinly to about 5 mm/¼ inch thick on a lightly floured work surface. Cut out shapes with a 6.5-cm/2½-inch snowflake- or star-shaped cutters and place on the baking sheets.

Bake in the preheated oven for 10–15 minutes, or until golden brown. Leave to cool on the baking sheets for 2–3 minutes, then transfer the cookies to a wire rack and leave to cool completely.

To make the icing, sift the icing sugar into a large bowl and add enough cold water to make a smooth, thick icing. Spread a little on each cookie and then sprinkle with sparkles and dragées.

29 Easter animal cookies

Use a rabbit-shaped cutter instead of a snowflake and add a raisin for the eyes. Alternatively, use a chick-shaped cutter and add a few drops of yellow food colouring to the icing.

225 g/8 oz butter, softened
140 g/5 oz caster sugar
1 egg yolk, lightly beaten
2 tsp vanilla extract
280 g/10 oz plain flour

pinch of salt
1 tsp ground ginger
1 tbsp finely grated orange rind
1 tbsp cocoa powder
1 egg white, lightly beaten

Place the butter and sugar in a large bowl and beat together until light and fluffy, then beat in the egg yolk and vanilla. Sift together the flour and salt into the mixture and stir until combined.

Divide the dough in half. Add the ginger and orange rind to one half and mix well. Shape the dough into a log 15 cm/6 inches long. Flatten the sides and top to square off the log to 5 cm/ 2 inches high. Wrap in clingfilm and chill for 30–60 minutes.

Sift the cocoa into the other half of the dough and mix well.

Shape into a flattened log exactly the same size as the first one, wrap in clingfilm and chill in the refrigerator for 30–60 minutes.

Unwrap the dough and cut each log lengthways into 3 slices. Cut each slice lengthways into 3 strips. Brush the strips with egg white and stack them in threes, alternating the colours, so they are the same shape as the original logs. Wrap in clingfilm and chill for 30–60 minutes.

Preheat the oven to 190°C/ 375°F/Gas Mark 5. Line 2 large baking sheets with baking paper.

Unwrap the logs and cut into slices with a sharp serrated knife, then place the cookies on the baking sheets, spaced well apart. Bake in the preheated oven for 12–15 minutes, or until firm. Leave to cool for 5–10 minutes, then transfer the cookies to wire racks to cool completely.

31 *Battenberg cookies*

Omit the orange rind and ginger. Use pink food colouring to tint one half of the dough and add cocoa to the other. Shape each dough portion into 2 logs and after chilling, cut each into 2 strips. Brush with egg white and stack a pink log on top of a chocolate one. Repeat and press the 4 pieces together into a rectangle. Wrap in clingfilm and chill. Cut into slices, then bake as before.

32 *Crunchy peanut biscuits*

MAKES 20

125 g/4½ oz butter, softened, plus extra
    for greasing
150 g/5½ oz chunky peanut butter
225 g/8 oz granulated sugar
1 egg, lightly beaten

150 g/5½ oz plain flour
½ tsp baking powder
pinch of salt
75 g/2¾ oz unsalted natural peanuts,
    chopped

Lightly grease 2 large baking sheets. Place the butter and peanut butter in a large bowl and beat together. Gradually add the sugar and beat together well. Add the egg, a little at a time, until it is combined. Sift the flour, baking powder and salt into the peanut butter mixture. Add the peanuts and bring all of the ingredients together to form a soft dough. Wrap the dough in clingfilm and chill in the refrigerator for 30 minutes.

Preheat the oven to 190°C/375°F/Gas Mark 5. Form the dough into 20 balls and place them on the baking sheets, about 5 cm/2 inches apart. Flatten them slightly with your hand.

Bake in the preheated oven for 15 minutes, or until golden brown. Leave to cool on wire racks.

225 g/8 oz plain flour, plus extra for dusting
150 g/5½ oz butter, cut into small pieces, plus extra for greasing
125 g/4½ oz caster sugar, plus extra for dusting
1 tsp vanilla extract

Preheat the oven to 180°C/350°F/Gas Mark 4. Grease a large baking sheet. Sift the flour into a large bowl, add the butter and rub it in with your fingertips until the mixture resembles fine breadcrumbs. Stir in the sugar and vanilla extract and mix together to form a firm dough.

Roll out the dough on a lightly floured work surface until it is 1 cm/½ inch thick. Cut out 12 hearts with a heart-shaped biscuit cutter measuring about 5 cm/2 inches across and arrange the hearts on the baking sheet.

Bake in the preheated oven for 15–20 minutes, or until just coloured. Transfer to a wire rack and leave to cool completely. Dust with a little caster sugar just before serving.

34   With vanilla topping

Beat 100 g/3½ oz unsalted butter with the seeds from a vanilla pod, sift in 150 g/5½ oz icing sugar and beat until smooth. Spread over the hearts.

35   Sugared hearts

225 g/8 oz butter, softened
280 g/10 oz caster sugar
1 egg yolk, lightly beaten
2 tsp vanilla extract
250 g/9 oz plain flour
25 g/1 oz cocoa powder
pinch of salt
3–4 food colouring pastes
100 g/3½ oz plain chocolate, broken into pieces

Place the butter and half the sugar in a large bowl and beat together until light and fluffy, then beat in the egg yolk and vanilla extract. Sift together the flour, cocoa and salt into the mixture and stir until combined. Halve the dough, shape into balls, wrap in clingfilm and chill for 30–60 minutes.

Preheat the oven to 190°C/375°F/Gas Mark 5. Line 2 large baking sheets with baking paper. Unwrap the dough and roll out between 2 sheets of baking paper. Cut out cookies with a heart-shaped cutter and place them on the baking sheets, spaced well apart. Bake in the preheated oven for 10–15 minutes, or until firm. Leave to cool on the baking sheets for 5–10 minutes, then transfer to wire racks to cool completely.

Meanwhile, divide the remaining sugar among 4 small plastic bags or bowls. Add a little food colouring paste to each and rub in until well mixed. Wear plastic gloves if mixing in bowls to prevent your hands from getting stained. Place the chocolate in a heatproof bowl, set the bowl over a saucepan of gently simmering water and heat until melted. Leave to cool slightly.

Leave the cookies on the racks. Spread the melted chocolate over them and sprinkle with the coloured sugar. Leave to set.

36   White sugar hearts

Replace the plain chocolate with white chocolate and sprinkle with desiccated coconut instead of the coloured sugar.

37 Painted ladies

2 sachets instant malted food drink
1 tbsp hot water
225 g/8 oz butter, softened
140 g/5 oz caster sugar
1 egg yolk, lightly beaten
280 g/10 oz plain flour

pinch of salt
egg yolk and food colouring, to decorate

Place the malted drink in a bowl and stir in the hot, but not boiling water to make a paste.

Place the butter and sugar in a large bowl and beat together until light and fluffy, then beat in the egg yolk and malted drink paste. Sift together the flour and salt into the mixture and stir until thoroughly combined. Halve the dough, shape into balls, wrap in clingfilm and chill in the refrigerator for 30–60 minutes.

Preheat the oven to 190°C/375°F/Gas Mark 5. Line 2 large baking sheets with baking paper. Unwrap the dough and roll out between 2 sheets of baking paper. Cut out cookies with a butterfly-shaped cutter and place them on the baking sheets.

Whisk an egg yolk and put a little of it in an egg cup. Add a few drops of food colouring and mix well. Using a fine paintbrush, paint a pattern on the butterflies' wings. Mix other colours with the beaten egg yolk in egg cups and add to the pattern.

Bake in the preheated oven for 10–15 minutes, or until firm. Leave to cool on the baking sheets for 5–10 minutes, then transfer the cookies to wire racks to cool completely.

38 Traffic lights

225 g/8 oz butter, softened
140 g/5 oz caster sugar
1 egg yolk, lightly beaten
280 g/10 oz plain flour, plus extra
for dusting
pinch of salt
100 g/3½ oz desiccated coconut

TO DECORATE
1½ tbsp lightly beaten egg white
1½ tbsp lemon juice
175 g/6 oz icing sugar
red, yellow and green glacé cherries
red and green gummy bears or
jelly babies

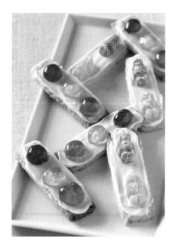

Place the butter and sugar in a large bowl and beat together until light and fluffy, then beat in the egg yolk and vanilla extract. Sift together the flour and salt into the mixture, add the coconut and stir until thoroughly combined. Halve the dough, roll each piece into a ball, wrap in clingfilm and chill for 30–60 minutes.

Preheat the oven to 190°C/375°F/Gas Mark 5. Line 2 large baking sheets with baking paper.

Roll out each piece of dough between 2 sheets of baking paper to a rectangle about 5 mm/¼ inch thick. Using a sharp knife, cut the dough into bars about 10 x 2-cm/4 x ¾-inches in size and place them on the baking sheets, spaced well apart. Bake in the preheated oven for 10–12 minutes, or until golden brown. Leave to cool on the baking sheets for 5–10 minutes, then transfer the cookies to wire racks to cool completely.

To make the icing, mix the egg white and lemon juice together in a bowl, then gradually beat in the icing sugar until smooth. Leave the cookies on the racks and spoon the icing over them. Decorate some with a vertical row of red, yellow and green glacé cherries for traffic lights. For pedestrian lights, put a red jelly baby or gummy bear at the top of a cookie and a green one at the bottom. Leave to set.

39 With jelly bean topping

Instead of the icing, place 150g/5½ oz plain chocolate in a heatproof bowl, set the bowl over a saucepan of gently simmering water and heat until melted. Spread the chocolate over the bars and press 3 jelly beans onto each.

350 g/12 oz plain flour, plus extra
    for dusting
pinch of salt
1 tsp bicarbonate of soda
100 g/3½ oz unsalted butter
175 g/6 oz caster sugar

1 large egg
1 tsp vanilla extract
4 tbsp golden syrup
50 mixed coloured boiled fruit sweets
    (about 250 g/9 oz), chopped
25 lengths of ribbon, to hang

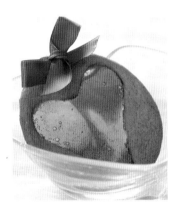

Sift the flour, salt and bicarbonate of soda into a large bowl, add the butter and rub it in until the mixture resembles breadcrumbs. Stir in the sugar. Place the egg, vanilla extract and golden syrup in a separate bowl and whisk together. Pour the egg into the flour mixture and mix to form a smooth dough. Wrap in clingfilm and chill in the refrigerator for 30 minutes.

Preheat the oven to 180°C/350°F/Gas Mark 4. Line 2 large baking sheets with baking paper. Roll the dough out on a floured work surface to 5 mm/¼ inch thick. Use a variety of floured cookie cutter shapes to cut out the biscuits.

Transfer them to the baking sheets and cut out shapes from the centre of the biscuits. Fill the holes with the sweets. Using a skewer, make a hole at the top of each biscuit.

Bake in the preheated oven for 10–12 minutes, or until the sweets are melted. Make sure the holes are still there, and re-pierce if necessary. Leave to cool on the baking sheets until the centres have hardened. When cold, thread thin ribbon through the holes to hang up the biscuits.

41 *Mint window cookies*

Cut all the cookies out with a round cookie cutter and use chopped, clear mint boiled sweets to fill the cavities. Hang using lengths of white ribbon.

42 *Chocolate dominoes*   MAKES ABOUT 28

225 g/8 oz butter, softened
140 g/5 oz caster sugar
1 egg yolk, lightly beaten
2 tsp vanilla extract
250 g/9 oz plain flour
25 g/1 oz cocoa powder
pinch of salt
25 g/1 oz desiccated coconut
50 g/1¾ oz white chocolate chips

Place the butter and sugar in a large bowl and beat together until light and fluffy, then beat in the egg yolk and vanilla extract. Sift together the flour, cocoa and salt into the mixture, add the coconut and stir until combined. Halve the dough, shape into balls, wrap in clingfilm and chill in the refrigerator for 30–60 minutes.

Preheat the oven to 190°C/375°F/Gas Mark 5. Line 2 large baking sheets with baking paper.

Unwrap the dough and roll out between 2 sheets of baking paper. Cut out biscuits with a 9-cm/3½-inch plain square cutter, then cut them in half to make rectangles. Place them on the baking sheets and, using a knife, make a line across the centre of each without cutting through. Arrange the chocolate chips on top of the biscuits to look like dominoes, pressing them in gently.

Bake in the preheated oven for 10–15 minutes, or until golden brown. Leave to cool for 5–10 minutes, then transfer to wire racks to cool completely.

43 *With black icing*

Sift 115 g/4 oz icing sugar into a bowl and beat in 1 tablespoon of water until smooth. Add a few drops of black food colouring and mix until black. Use to ice the cookies, leave to set, then add the white dots with white writing icing.

44 Double heart cookies

1 sachet instant latte
1½ tsp hot water
225 g/8 oz butter, softened
140 g/5 oz caster sugar
1 egg yolk, lightly beaten

250 g/9 oz plain flour
1 tsp vanilla extract
3 tbsp cocoa powder
pinch of salt

Place the instant latte into a small bowl and stir in the hot, but not boiling, water to make a paste.

Place the butter and sugar in a large bowl and beat together until light and fluffy, then beat in the egg yolk. Divide the mixture in half. Beat the latte paste into one half. Sift 140 g/5 oz of the flour with the salt into the mixture and stir until combined. Shape the dough into a ball, wrap in clingfilm and chill in the refrigerator for 30–60 minutes. Beat the vanilla extract into the other bowl, then sift together the remaining flour, the cocoa powder and salt into the mixture. Stir until thoroughly combined. Shape the dough into a ball, wrap in clingfilm and chill for 30–60 minutes.

Preheat the oven to 190°C/375°F/Gas Mark 5. Line 2 large baking sheets with baking paper. Unwrap both flavours of dough and roll out each between 2 sheets of baking paper. Cut out cookies with a 7-cm/2¾-inch heart-shaped cutter and place them on the baking sheets, spaced well apart. Using a 4–5-cm/1½–2-inch heart-shaped cutter, cut out the centres of each larger heart and remove from the baking sheets. Place a small chocolate-flavoured heart in the centre of each large coffee-flavoured heart and vice versa.

Bake in the preheated oven for 10–15 minutes. Leave to cool for 5–10 minutes, then transfer to wire racks to cool completely.

45 Pink hearts

Divide the dough into 3 portions and add pink food colouring to one portion, then make the cookies as before, contrasting the 3 different coloured doughs.

46 Chocolate-dipped Viennese fingers

100 g/3½ oz butter, plus extra for greasing
25 g/1 oz golden caster sugar

½ tsp vanilla extract
100 g/3½ oz self-raising flour
100 g/3½ oz plain chocolate

Preheat the oven to 160°C/325°F/Gas Mark 3. Grease 2 large baking sheets. Place the butter, sugar and vanilla extract in a large bowl and beat together until light and fluffy. Stir in the flour, mixing evenly to make a fairly stiff dough.

Place the mixture in a piping bag fitted with a large star nozzle and pipe about 16 fingers, each 6 cm/2½ inches long, onto the baking sheets. Bake in the preheated oven for 10–15 minutes, or until pale golden. Leave to cool on the baking sheets for 2–3 minutes, then transfer to a wire rack to cool completely.

Place the chocolate in a small heatproof bowl, set over a saucepan of gently simmering water and heat until melted. Remove from the heat. Dip the ends of each biscuit into the chocolate to coat, then place on a sheet of baking paper and leave to set.

47 Viennese pinks

Omit the chocolate and dip each end of the fingers into pink icing made by beating 115 g/4 oz sifted icing sugar with 1 tablespoon of water and a drop of pink food colouring. Before the icing is dry, dip the tips into pink sparkles, then leave to set.

48 *Alphabet cookies*

225 g/8 oz butter, softened
140 g/5 oz caster sugar
1 egg yolk, lightly beaten
2 tsp grenadine
280 g/10 oz plain flour

pinch of salt
5–6 tbsp unsalted dried pomegranate
seeds or roasted melon seeds

Place the butter and sugar in a large bowl and beat together until light and fluffy, then beat in the egg yolk and grenadine. Sift together the flour and salt into the mixture and stir until combined. Halve the dough, shape into balls, wrap in clingfilm and chill for 30–60 minutes.

Preheat the oven to 190°C/375°F/Gas Mark 5. Line 2 large baking sheets with baking paper.

Unwrap the dough and roll out between 2 sheets of baking paper to about 3 mm/⅛ inch thick. Sprinkle half the seeds over each piece of dough and lightly roll the rolling pin over them. Cut out letters with alphabet cutters and place them on the baking sheets, spaced well apart.

Bake in the preheated oven for 10–12 minutes, or until golden brown. Leave to cool on the baking sheets for 5–10 minutes, then transfer the cookies to wire racks to cool completely.

49 *Tutti frutti cookies*

Replace the seeds with 25 g/1 oz each of chopped candied fruit, glacé cherries and angelica and add to the cookie dough.

50 *Iced stars*

225 g/8 oz butter, softened
140 g/5 oz caster sugar
1 egg yolk, lightly beaten
½ tsp vanilla extract
280 g/10 oz plain flour
pinch of salt

TO DECORATE
200 g/7 oz icing sugar
1–2 tbsp warm water
food colourings
silver and gold dragées
hundreds and thousands
desiccated coconut
sugar sprinkles
sugar stars, hearts and flowers

Place the butter and sugar in a large bowl and beat together until light and fluffy, then beat in the egg yolk and vanilla extract. Sift together the flour and salt into the mixture and stir until thoroughly combined. Halve the dough, shape into balls, wrap in clingfilm and chill for 30–60 minutes.

Preheat the oven to 190°C/375°F/Gas Mark 5. Line 2 large baking sheets with baking paper.

Unwrap the dough and roll out between 2 sheets of baking paper to about 3 mm/⅛ inch thick. Cut out cookies with a star-shaped cutter and place them on the baking sheets, spaced well apart. Bake in the preheated oven for 10–15 minutes, or until light golden brown. Leave to cool on the baking sheets for 5–10 minutes, then transfer to wire racks to cool completely.

To decorate, sift the icing sugar into a bowl and stir in enough warm water until it is the consistency of thick cream. Divide the icing among 3–4 bowls and add a few drops of your chosen food colourings to each. Leave the cookies on the racks and spread the different coloured icings over them to the edges. Arrange silver and gold dragées on top and/or sprinkle with hundreds and thousands and sugar shapes. If you like, colour desiccated coconut with food colouring in a contrasting colour. Leave the cookies to set.

51 *Marzipan stars*

Omit the icing and thinly roll 150 g/5½ oz white marzipan out on a work surface dusted with icing sugar. Cut out 30 stars with the star-shaped cutter and use a little beaten egg white to secure the marzipan to the cookies, then use a kitchen blow torch to toast the edges of the marzipan.

125 g/4½ oz butter, softened
175 g/6 oz caster sugar
1 egg, lightly beaten
½ tsp vanilla extract
125 g/4½ oz plain flour
35 g/1¼ oz cocoa powder
½ tsp bicarbonate of soda

Preheat the oven to 180°C/350°F/
Gas Mark 4. Line several large
baking sheets with baking paper.

Place the butter and sugar in
a large bowl and beat together
until light and fluffy. Add the egg
and vanilla extract and mix until
smooth. Sift in the flour, cocoa
and bicarbonate of soda and beat
until well mixed.

With dampened hands, roll
walnut-sized pieces of the dough
into smooth balls. Place on the
baking sheets, spaced well apart.

Bake in the preheated oven for
10–12 minutes, or until set. Leave
to cool on the baking sheets for
5 minutes, then transfer the
cookies to wire racks to cool
completely before serving.

53 *With chocolate topping*

*As the cookies cool, put 75 g/2¾ oz plain chocolate in a heatproof bowl, set
the bowl over a saucepan of gently simmering water and heat until melted.
Remove from the heat and stir until smooth. Spoon the chocolate into a
piping bag fitted with a writing nozzle and drizzle the chocolate over the
cookies in a decorative zigzag pattern, then leave to set.*

54 *Sugar-coated midnight cookies*

*Sprinkle 50 g/1¾ oz granulated sugar on a large plate. Roll each ball
of dough in the sugar to coat before placing on the baking sheets.*

56 Cherry refrigerator cookies

Finely chop 100 g/3½ oz glacé cherries and add to the mixture with the caster sugar.

57 Chocolate refrigerator cookies

Finely grate 100 g/3½ oz plain chocolate and add to the mixture with the caster sugar.

58 Coconut refrigerator cookies

Add 100 g/3½ oz desiccated coconut to the mixture with the caster sugar.

59 Dried fruit refrigerator cookies

Finely chop 100 g/3½ oz sultanas, raisins or cranberries and add to the mixture with the caster sugar.

60 Ginger refrigerator cookies

Omit the vanilla extract and sift 3 teaspoons of ground ginger into the mixture with the flour.

61 Lemon refrigerator cookies

Omit the vanilla extract and finely grate the rind of 2 lemons into the mixture with the caster sugar.

62 Orange refrigerator cookies

Omit the vanilla extract and finely grate the rind of 2 oranges into the mixture with the caster sugar.

63 Spicy refrigerator cookies

Omit the vanilla extract and sift 4 teaspoons of ground mixed spice into the mixture with the flour.

64 Walnut refrigerator cookies

Chop 100 g/3½ oz walnut halves and add to the mixture with the caster sugar.

---

450 g/1 lb plain flour, plus extra for dusting
2 tsp baking powder
225 g/8 oz butter, cut into cubes, plus extra for greasing

350 g/12 oz caster sugar
2 large eggs, lightly beaten
2 tsp vanilla extract

Sift the flour and baking powder into a large bowl. Add the butter and rub it in with your fingertips until the mixture resembles fine breadcrumbs. Stir the sugar into the mixture, add the eggs and vanilla extract and mix together to form a soft dough.

Turn the mixture onto a lightly floured work surface and divide the dough in half. Shape each piece of dough into a log shape about 6 cm/2½ inches thick. Wrap each log in baking paper and then in foil and chill in the refrigerator for at least 8 hours, or until required.

Preheat the oven to 190°C/375°F/Gas Mark 5. Grease several large baking sheets. Slice the dough into as many 8-mm/³⁄₈-inch slices as required and place on the baking sheets, spaced well apart. Return any remaining dough to the refrigerator for up to 1 week, or to the freezer until required. Bake in the preheated oven for 10–15 minutes, or until golden brown. Leave on the baking sheet to cool slightly for 2–3 minutes, then transfer the cookies to a wire rack to cool completely.

250 g/9 oz unsalted butter, softened
275 g/9¾ oz caster sugar
2 large eggs, lightly beaten
450 g/1 lb plain flour, plus extra
for dusting
2 tsp baking powder
pinch of salt
few drops of food colouring
writing icing

Place the butter and sugar in a large bowl and beat together until light and fluffy. Gradually add the eggs and beat to combine, then sift in the flour, baking powder and salt and mix to form a dough. Wrap the dough in clingfilm and chill in the refrigerator for 2 hours.

Preheat the oven to 160°C/ 325°F/Gas Mark 3. Line 2 large baking sheets with baking paper.

Reserve one third of the dough and leave uncoloured. Divide the remaining dough into portions and knead in different food colourings. Shape the dough into animal shapes (see right) and

place the cookies on the baking sheets. Bake for 20–25 minutes. Leave to cool on a wire rack. Add eyes and other features with the writing icing.

Cow Cookie: shape an oval piece of coloured dough to 6 cm/ 2½ inches across for the body. Roll another piece of dough into a log 6 cm/2½ inches long and 1 cm/½ inch wide, then cut into 3 equal pieces – use 2 for the legs and 1 for the head. Roll uncoloured dough into small circles and use as the udder, nose and markings. Make a thin tail. Press the pieces well together.

Pig Cookie: shape an oval piece of coloured dough to 6 cm/ 2½ inches across for the body; flatten. Shape a smaller oval piece to 3 cm/1¼ inches for the head; flatten. Use uncoloured dough for the snout, ears and tail.

Fluffy Sheep Cookie: for the body, roll small balls of uncoloured dough and lay them on the baking sheet, touching each other in an oval shape. Use coloured dough to shape the head and feet.

100 g/3½ oz butter
100 g/3½ oz soft light brown sugar
1 tbsp golden syrup

150 g/5½ oz self-raising flour
85 g/3 oz sugar-coated chocolates

Preheat the oven to 180°C/350°F/Gas Mark 4. Line several large baking sheets with baking paper. Place the butter and sugar in a large bowl and whisk together until pale and creamy, then whisk the golden syrup into the mixture until smooth. Add 75 g/2¾ oz flour and whisk together until mixed. Stir in the sugar-coated chocolates and remaining flour, then, with your hands, knead the mixture until smooth.

Roll small pieces of the dough between your hands into smooth balls to make 15 cookies in total and place them on the baking sheets, spacing them well apart. Bake in the preheated oven for 10–15 minutes, or until golden brown.

Leave on the baking sheets for 2–3 minutes, then transfer the cookies to a wire rack and leave to cool completely.

67 *Choco mint stars*

225 g/8 oz butter, softened
140 g/5 oz caster sugar
1 egg yolk, lightly beaten
1 tsp peppermint extract
280 g/10 oz plain flour
pinch of salt
100 g/3½ oz desiccated coconut

TO DECORATE
100 g/3½ oz white chocolate, broken
   into pieces
100 g/3½ oz milk chocolate, broken
   into pieces

Place the butter and sugar in a large bowl and beat together until light and fluffy, then beat in the egg yolk and peppermint extract. Sift together the flour and salt into the mixture, add the coconut and stir until combined. Divide the mixture in half, shape into balls, wrap in clingfilm and chill in the refrigerator for 30–60 minutes.

Preheat the oven to 190°C/375°F/Gas Mark 5. Line 2 large baking sheets with baking paper. Unwrap the dough and roll out between 2 sheets of baking paper to about 3 mm/⅛ inch thick.

Cut out stars with a 6–7-cm/2½–2¾-inch cutter and place them on the baking sheets, spaced well apart.

Bake in the preheated oven for 10–12 minutes, or until light golden. Leave to cool on the baking sheets for 5–10 minutes, then transfer the cookies to wire racks to cool completely.

Place the white chocolate and the milk chocolate in separate heatproof bowls, set the bowls over 2 saucepans of gently simmering water and heat until melted. Leave the cooled cookies on the racks and drizzle first with melted white chocolate and then with melted milk chocolate, using a teaspoon. Leave to set.

68 *White mint stars*

Omit the milk chocolate and melt 200 g/7 oz white chocolate in a heatproof bowl set over a pan of gently simmering water. Spread to cover each cookie and sprinkle over chocolate vermicelli.

225 g/8 oz butter, softened
140 g/5 oz caster sugar
1 egg yolk, lightly beaten
2 tsp vanilla extract
225 g/8 oz plain flour
55 g/2 oz cocoa powder

pinch of salt
about 90 white mini marshmallows,
    halved horizontally
4 tbsp peach jam
4 tbsp yellow sugar sprinkles

Place the butter and sugar in a large bowl and beat together until light and fluffy, then beat in the egg yolk and vanilla extract.

Sift together the flour, cocoa and salt into the mixture and stir until thoroughly combined. Halve the dough, roll each piece into a ball, wrap in clingfilm and chill in the refrigerator for 30–60 minutes.

Preheat the oven to 190°C/ 375°F/Gas Mark 5. Line 2 large baking sheets with baking paper.

Unwrap the dough and roll out between 2 sheets of baking paper to about 1 cm/½ inch thick. Cut out 30 cookies with a 5-cm/2-inch flower cookie cutter and put them on the baking sheets, making sure they are spaced well apart.

Bake in the preheated oven for 10–12 minutes, or until firm. Remove from the oven but do not turn off the heat. Arrange the pieces of marshmallow over the petals of the flowers, cutting them to fit if necessary. Return to the

oven for 30–60 seconds, or until the marshmallow has softened.

Leave to cool on the baking sheets for 5–10 minutes, then transfer the cookies to wire racks to cool completely. Meanwhile, heat the jam in a small saucepan, strain into a bowl and leave to cool. Pipe a small circle of jam in the centre of each flower and top with the sugar sprinkles.

85 *Chocolate button daisies*

Omit the cocoa powder from the dough mixture and use chocolate buttons instead of the marshmallows.

86 *Chocolate florentines*

50 g/1¾ oz unsalted butter
50 g/1¾ oz caster sugar
50 g/1¾ oz golden syrup
50 g/1¾ oz plain flour

25 g/1 oz glacé cherries, chopped
50 g/1¾ oz flaked almonds
50 g/1¾ oz candied peel, chopped
175 g/6 oz plain chocolate, chopped

Preheat the oven to 180°C/350°F/Gas Mark 4. Line 2 large baking sheets with baking paper. Heat the butter, sugar and golden syrup together in a saucepan over a low heat until the butter is melted and the sugar is dissolved. Stir in the flour, cherries, almonds and candied peel.

Make the florentines in batches: place heaped teaspoons of the mixture on the baking sheets, spaced well apart, and flatten slightly with the back of a spoon. Bake in the preheated oven for 8–10 minutes, or until golden brown. Leave to cool on the baking sheets for 2–3 minutes, then transfer to a wire rack and leave until cold. Repeat until you have 20 florentines.

Place the chocolate in a heatproof bowl, set the bowl over a saucepan of gently simmering water and heat until melted. Using a pastry brush, spread the chocolate over the base of each florentine and place chocolate side up on a wire rack to cool and set.

87 *Ginger florentines*

Replace the glacé cherries and candied peel with 85 g/3 oz chopped crystallized ginger.

Lemon & lime cookies

140 g/5 oz plain chocolate, broken into
   pieces, to decorate
30 thinly pared strips of lime rind, to
   decorate
225 g/8 oz butter, softened
140 g/5 oz caster sugar
1 egg yolk, lightly beaten
2 tsp lime juice

280 g/10 oz plain flour
pinch of salt
finely grated rind of 1 lemon

ICING
1 tbsp lightly beaten egg white
1 tbsp lime juice
115 g/4 oz icing sugar

To make the decoration, place the chocolate in a heatproof bowl, set the bowl over a saucepan of gently simmering water and heat until melted. Leave to cool slightly. Line a baking sheet with baking paper. Dip the strips of lime rind into the chocolate until coated, then put on the baking sheet to set.

Place the butter and sugar in a large bowl and beat together until light and fluffy, then beat in the egg yolk and lime juice. Sift together the flour and salt into the mixture, add the lemon rind and stir until combined. Halve the dough, shape into balls, wrap in clingfilm and chill in the refrigerator for 30–60 minutes.

Preheat the oven to 190°C/ 375°F/Gas Mark 5. Line 2 large baking sheets with baking paper. Unwrap the dough and roll out between 2 sheets of baking paper to about 3 mm/⅛ inch thick. Cut out rounds with a 6-cm/2½-inch plain cutter and place them on the baking sheets. Bake in the preheated oven for 10–15 minutes, or until golden brown. Leave to cool on the baking sheets for 5–10 minutes, then transfer to wire racks to cool completely.

To make the icing, place the egg white and lime juice in a bowl and mix together, then gradually beat in the icing sugar until smooth. Ice the cookies and top with the chocolate-coated lime rind. Leave to set.

81 *With plain chocolate topping*

Omit the lime rind and simply drizzle the melted plain chocolate over the icing and leave to set.

Lemon & sesame seed cookies

2 tbsp sesame seeds
225 g/8 oz butter, softened
140 g/5 oz caster sugar
1 tbsp finely grated lemon rind
1 egg yolk, lightly beaten
280 g/10 oz plain flour
pinch of salt

ICING
115 g/4 oz icing sugar
few drops of lemon extract
1 tbsp hot water

Dry-fry the sesame seeds in a heavy-based frying pan over a low heat, stirring frequently, for 2–3 minutes, or until they give off their aroma. Leave to cool.

Place the butter, sugar, lemon rind and toasted seeds in a large bowl and beat together until light and fluffy, then beat in the egg yolk. Sift together the flour and salt into the mixture and stir until combined. Halve the dough, form it into balls, wrap in clingfilm and chill in the refrigerator for 30–60 minutes.

Preheat the oven to 190°C/ 375°F/Gas Mark 5. Line 2 large baking sheets with baking paper. Unwrap the dough and roll out between 2 sheets of baking paper. Cut out rounds with a 6-cm/ 2½-inch cutter and place them on the baking sheets, spaced well apart. Bake in the preheated oven for 10–12 minutes, or until light golden brown. Leave to cool on the baking sheets for 5–10 minutes, then transfer the cookies to wire racks to cool completely.

To make the icing, sift the icing sugar into a bowl, add the lemon extract and gradually stir in the hot water until the icing is smooth and has the consistency of thick cream. Leave the cooled cookies on the racks and spread the icing over them. Leave to set.

83 *Lime & sesame seed cookies*

Omit the lemon in this recipe and replace with lime, then top the icing with finely grated lime rind.

225 g/8 oz butter, softened
140 g/5 oz caster sugar
1 egg yolk, lightly beaten
2 tsp vanilla extract
225 g/8 oz plain flour
55 g/2 oz cocoa powder

pinch of salt
about 90 white mini marshmallows,
    halved horizontally
4 tbsp peach jam
4 tbsp yellow sugar sprinkles

Place the butter and sugar in a large bowl and beat together until light and fluffy, then beat in the egg yolk and vanilla extract.

Sift together the flour, cocoa and salt into the mixture and stir until thoroughly combined. Halve the dough, roll each piece into a ball, wrap in clingfilm and chill in the refrigerator for 30–60 minutes.

Preheat the oven to 190°C/375°F/Gas Mark 5. Line 2 large baking sheets with baking paper.

Unwrap the dough and roll out between 2 sheets of baking paper to about 1 cm/½ inch thick. Cut out 30 cookies with a 5-cm/2-inch flower cookie cutter and put them on the baking sheets, making sure they are spaced well apart.

Bake in the preheated oven for 10–12 minutes, or until firm. Remove from the oven but do not turn off the heat. Arrange the pieces of marshmallow over the petals of the flowers, cutting them to fit if necessary. Return to the oven for 30–60 seconds, or until the marshmallow has softened.

Leave to cool on the baking sheets for 5–10 minutes, then transfer the cookies to wire racks to cool completely. Meanwhile, heat the jam in a small saucepan, strain into a bowl and leave to cool. Pipe a small circle of jam in the centre of each flower and top with the sugar sprinkles.

85 *Chocolate button daisies*

Omit the cocoa powder from the dough mixture and use chocolate buttons instead of the marshmallows.

86 *Chocolate florentines*

50 g/1¾ oz unsalted butter
50 g/1¾ oz caster sugar
50 g/1¾ oz golden syrup
50 g/1¾ oz plain flour

25 g/1 oz glacé cherries, chopped
50 g/1¾ oz flaked almonds
50 g/1¾ oz candied peel, chopped
175 g/6 oz plain chocolate, chopped

Preheat the oven to 180°C/350°F/Gas Mark 4. Line 2 large baking sheets with baking paper. Heat the butter, sugar and golden syrup together in a saucepan over a low heat until the butter is melted and the sugar is dissolved. Stir in the flour, cherries, almonds and candied peel.

Make the florentines in batches: place heaped teaspoons of the mixture on the baking sheets, spaced well apart, and flatten slightly with the back of a spoon. Bake in the preheated oven for 8–10 minutes, or until golden brown. Leave to cool on the baking sheets for 2–3 minutes, then transfer to a wire rack and leave until cold. Repeat until you have 20 florentines.

Place the chocolate in a heatproof bowl, set the bowl over a saucepan of gently simmering water and heat until melted. Using a pastry brush, spread the chocolate over the base of each florentine and place chocolate side up on a wire rack to cool and set.

87 *Ginger florentines*

Replace the glacé cherries and candied peel with 85 g/3 oz chopped crystallized ginger.

Whirly pinwheel cookies

100 g/3½ oz unsalted butter, softened
50 g/1¾ oz caster sugar
50 g/1¾ oz cornflour
100 g/3½ oz plain flour, plus 1 tbsp
   for dusting

1 large egg yolk
1 tbsp milk
2 tbsp cocoa powder

Place the butter and sugar in a large bowl and beat together until light and fluffy. Sift in the cornflour and the flour and mix well to combine, then add the egg yolk and a little milk to form a stiff dough.

Divide the dough mixture in half, add the cocoa powder to one half and mix well together. Wrap both doughs in clingfilm and chill in the refrigerator for 30 minutes.

Roll each piece of dough into a rectangle 3 mm/⅛ inch thick. Lay the chocolate dough on top of the white dough, then press together and trim the edges. Roll up lengthways, wrap tightly in clingfilm and chill in the refrigerator for 30 minutes.

Preheat the oven to 180°C/ 350°F/Gas Mark 4. Unwrap the dough and cut across the roll into 20 slices, then place the cookies on a non-stick baking sheet. Bake in the preheated oven for 15–20 minutes. Leave to cool on a wire rack.

89 *Hazelnut whirly pinwheel cookies*

Add 3 tablespoons of finely chopped hazelnuts to the chocolate dough and knead in before chilling the dough.

90 *Good-for-you wholemeal biscuits*

300 g/10½ oz plain wholemeal flour,
   plus extra for dusting
2 tbsp wheatgerm
¼ tsp bicarbonate of soda
½ tsp salt

50 g/1¾ oz caster sugar
125 g/4½ oz unsalted butter, cubed
1 large egg, lightly beaten
1 tsp vanilla extract

Preheat the oven to 170°C/325°F/Gas Mark 3. Place the flour, wheatgerm, bicarbonate of soda, salt and sugar in a large bowl and stir together until combined. Add the butter and rub it in until the mixture resembles breadcrumbs.

Whisk the egg and vanilla extract in a separate bowl and add to the mixture, adding a little cold water if needed to bring the dough together. Roll the dough out on a floured board. Use a 7-cm/2¾-inch floured cookie cutter to cut out the biscuits and place them on non-stick baking sheets, re-rolling the dough when necessary.

Bake in batches in the preheated oven for 20–25 minutes, or until dry but not brown. Leave to cool on a wire rack.

91 *Fruit wholemeal biscuits*

Knead 2 tablespoons of chopped currants or chopped mixed peel and ½ teaspoon of mixed ground spice into the dough before rolling out.

55 g/2 oz raisins, chopped
125 ml/4 fl oz orange juice
225 g/8 oz butter, softened
140 g/5 oz caster sugar
1 egg yolk, lightly beaten
2 tsp vanilla extract

225 g/8 oz plain flour
pinch of salt
55 g/2 oz rolled oats
55 g/2 oz hazelnuts, chopped
about 30 whole hazelnut

Preheat the oven to 190°C/375°F/Gas Mark 5. Line 2 large baking sheets with baking paper. Place the raisins in a bowl, add the orange juice and leave to soak for 10 minutes.

Place the butter and sugar in a large bowl and beat together until light and fluffy, then beat in the egg yolk and vanilla extract. Sift together the flour and salt into the mixture and add the oats and hazelnuts. Drain the raisins, add them to the mixture and stir until combined. Scoop up tablespoons of the mixture and place them in mounds on the baking sheets, spaced well apart. Flatten slightly and place a whole hazelnut in the centre of each cookie.

Bake in the preheated oven for 12–15 minutes, or until golden brown. Leave to cool on the baking sheets for 5–10 minutes, then transfer to wire racks to cool completely.

93 *Oaty sultana & walnut cookies*

Replace the raisins and hazelnuts with 55 g/2 oz chopped sultanas and 100 g/3½ oz chopped walnuts.

94 *Lemon polenta cookies* MAKES 12

100 g/3½ oz butter, softened
70 g/2½ oz caster sugar
2 large eggs, lightly beaten
finely grated rind of 1 lemon
1 tbsp lemon juice

150 g/5½ oz plain flour
70 g/2½ oz polenta
12 whole blanched almonds

Preheat the oven to 190°C/375°F/Gas Mark 5. Line several large baking sheets with baking paper. Place the butter and sugar in a large bowl and whisk until pale and creamy. Whisk the beaten eggs, lemon rind and juice into the mixture until smooth, then add the flour and polenta and beat together until mixed.

Place the mixture in a piping bag fitted with a plain 2-cm/¾-inch nozzle. Pipe swirls, measuring about 6 cm/2½ inches in diameter, onto the baking sheets, spaced well apart, and top each cookie with a blanched almond.

Bake in the preheated oven for 10–15 minutes, or until lightly golden brown. Leave to cool on the baking sheets for 5 minutes, then transfer the cookies to a wire rack to cool completely.

Orange & chocolate fingers

225 g/8 oz butter, softened
140 g/5 oz caster sugar
finely grated rind of 1 orange
1 egg yolk, lightly beaten
2 tsp orange juice

280 g/10 oz plain flour
1 tsp ground ginger
pinch of salt
115 g/4 oz plain chocolate, broken into
pieces

Place the butter, sugar and orange rind in a large bowl and beat together until light and fluffy, then beat in the egg yolk and orange juice. Sift together the flour, ginger and salt into the mixture and stir until combined. Shape the dough into a ball, wrap in clingfilm and chill in the refrigerator for 30–60 minutes.

Preheat the oven to 190°C/375°F/Gas Mark 5. Line 2 large baking sheets with baking paper. Unwrap the dough and roll out between 2 sheets of baking paper to a rectangle. Using a sharp knife, cut it into 10 x 2-cm/4 x ¾-inch strips and place them on the baking sheets, spaced well apart.

Bake in the preheated oven for 10–12 minutes, or until light golden brown. Leave to cool for 5–10 minutes, then transfer to wire racks to cool completely.

Place the chocolate in a heatproof bowl, set the bowl over a saucepan of gently simmering water and heat until melted, then leave to cool. When the chocolate is cool but not set, dip the cookies diagonally into it to half coat, then place on the wire racks to set. You may find it easier to do this with tongs.

96 Lemon & white chocolate fingers

Replace the orange rind and juice with lemon and use melted white chocolate to half-coat the cookies.

---

97 Orange & lemon cookies

225 g/8 oz butter, softened
140 g/5 oz caster sugar
1 egg yolk, lightly beaten
280 g/10 oz plain flour
pinch of salt
finely grated rind of 1 orange
finely grated rind of 1 lemon

TO DECORATE
1 tbsp lightly beaten egg white
1 tbsp lemon juice
115 g/4 oz icing sugar
few drops of yellow food colouring
few drops of orange food colouring
about 15 lemon jelly slices
about 15 orange jelly slices

Place the butter and sugar in a large bowl and beat together until light and fluffy, then beat in the egg yolk. Sift together the flour and salt into the mixture and stir until combined. Halve the dough and knead the orange rind into one half and the lemon rind into the other. Shape into balls, wrap and chill for 30–60 minutes.

Preheat the oven to 190°C/375°F/Gas Mark 5. Line 2 large baking sheets with baking paper. Unwrap the orange-flavoured dough and roll out between 2 sheets of baking paper. Cut out rounds with a 6-cm/2½-inch plain cutter and place them on a baking sheet, spaced well apart. Repeat with the lemon-flavoured dough and cut-out crescents. Place them on the other baking sheet, spaced well apart.

Bake in the preheated oven for 10–15 minutes, or until golden brown. Leave to cool for 5–10 minutes, then transfer to wire racks to cool completely.

To decorate, mix the egg white and lemon juice together. Gradually beat in the icing sugar until smooth. Spoon half the icing into another bowl. Stir yellow food colouring into one bowl and orange into the other. Leave the cookies on the racks. Spread the icing over the cookies and decorate with jelly slices. Leave to set.

98 Raspberry cookies

Omit the citrus rind from the dough and replace the orange and yellow food colouring with red food colouring. Top the cookies with raspberry jelly slices.

99 *Banana & caramel cookies*

225 g/8 oz butter, softened
140 g/5 oz caster sugar
1 egg yolk, lightly beaten
25 g/1 oz stem ginger, finely chopped,
    plus 2 tsp syrup from the jar

280 g/10 oz plain flour
pinch of salt
85 g/3 oz dried bananas, finely chopped
15 chocolate caramels

Place the butter and sugar in a large bowl and beat together until light and fluffy, then beat in the egg yolk, ginger and ginger syrup. Sift together the flour and salt into the mixture, add the bananas and stir until thoroughly combined. Halve the dough, shape into balls, wrap in clingfilm and chill in the refrigerator for 30–60 minutes.

Preheat the oven to 190°C/375°F/Gas Mark 5. Line 2 large baking sheets with baking paper. Then unwrap the dough and roll it out between 2 sheets of baking paper. Cut out cookies with a 6-cm/ 2½-inch fluted round cutter and place half of them on the baking sheets, spaced well apart. Place a chocolate caramel in the centre of each cookie, then top with the remaining cookies and pinch the edges of the rounds together.

Bake in the preheated oven for 10–15 minutes, or until light golden. Cool for 5–10 minutes, then transfer to wire racks to cool completely.

100 *Banana & raisin cookies*

25 g/1 oz raisins
125 ml/4 fl oz orange juice or rum
225 g/8 oz butter, softened
140 g/5 oz caster sugar
1 egg yolk, lightly beaten

280 g/10 oz plain flour
pinch of salt
85 g/3 oz dried bananas, finely chopped

Place the raisins in a bowl, pour in the orange juice or rum and leave to soak for 30 minutes. Drain the raisins, reserving any remaining liquid.

Preheat the oven to 190°C/375°F/Gas Mark 5. Line 2 large baking sheets with baking paper. Place the butter and sugar in a large bowl and beat together until light and fluffy, then beat in the egg yolk and 2 teaspoons of the reserved orange juice. Sift together the flour and salt into the mixture, add the raisins and dried bananas and stir until combined.

Place tablespoons of the mixture into heaps on the baking sheets, spaced well apart, then flatten them gently.

Bake in the preheated oven for 12–15 minutes, or until golden. Leave to cool on the baking sheets for 5–10 minutes, then transfer the cookies to wire racks to cool completely.

101 *Banana & coconut cookies*

Replace the raisins with 50 g/1¾ oz desiccated coconut.

225 g/8 oz butter, softened
140 g/5 oz caster sugar
2 tsp finely grated orange rind
1 egg yolk, lightly beaten
2 tsp vanilla extract
250 g/9 oz plain flour
25 g/1 oz cocoa powder
pinch of salt
100 g/3½ oz plain chocolate,
finely chopped

CHOCOLATE FILLING
125 ml/4 fl oz double cream
200 g/7 oz white chocolate,
broken into pieces
1 tsp orange extract

Preheat the oven to 190°C/375°F/ Gas Mark 5. Line 2 large baking sheets with baking paper.

Place the butter, sugar and orange rind in a large bowl and beat together until light and fluffy. Beat in the egg yolk and vanilla. Sift together the flour, cocoa and salt into the mixture, then add the chocolate and stir well. Scoop up tablespoons of the dough, roll into balls and place on the baking sheets, spaced well apart. Gently flatten and smooth the tops with the back of a spoon.

Bake in the preheated oven for 10–15 minutes, or until light golden. Leave to cool on the baking sheets for 5–10 minutes, then transfer to wire racks to cool completely.

To make the filling, bring the cream to the boil in a small saucepan, then remove the pan from the heat. Stir in the chocolate until the mixture is smooth, then stir in the orange extract. When the mixture is completely cool, sandwich the cookies together in pairs.

103   *With plain chocolate*

For the chocolate filling, replace the white chocolate with plain chocolate and sift over cocoa powder to finish.

104   *With plain & white chocolate*

Replace half the white chocolate with melted plain chocolate to make 2 fillings. Fill half the sandwiches with white filling and sift over icing sugar. Fill the remaining cookies with plain chocolate filling and sift over cocoa powder.

105 *Snickerdoodles*

225 g/8 oz butter, softened
140 g/5 oz caster sugar
2 large eggs, lightly beaten
1 tsp vanilla extract
400 g/14 oz plain flour
1 tsp bicarbonate of soda
½ tsp freshly grated nutmeg

pinch of salt
55 g/2 oz pecan nuts, finely chopped

CINNAMON COATING
1 tbsp caster sugar
2 tbsp ground cinnamon

Place the butter and sugar in a large bowl and beat together until light and fluffy, then beat in the eggs and vanilla extract. Sift together the flour, bicarbonate of soda, nutmeg and salt into the mixture, add the pecan nuts and stir until thoroughly combined. Shape the dough into a ball, wrap in clingfilm and chill in the refrigerator for 30–60 minutes.

Preheat the oven to 190°C/375°F/Gas Mark 5. Line 2 large baking sheets with baking paper.

For the coating, mix the sugar and cinnamon in a shallow dish. Scoop up tablespoons of the dough and roll into balls. Roll each ball in the cinnamon mixture and place on the baking sheets, spaced well apart. Bake in the preheated oven for 10–12 minutes, or until golden brown. Cool for 5–10 minutes, then transfer to wire racks to cool completely.

106 *Chocodoodles*

Add 2 tablespoons of cocoa powder to the dough and roll the cookies in 2 tablespoons of caster sugar mixed with 1 tablespoon of cocoa before baking.

107 *Melt-in-the-middles*

85 g/3 oz plain chocolate, broken into
    pieces
115 g/4 oz butter, softened
140 g/5 oz caster sugar
1 egg yolk, lightly beaten
2 tsp vanilla extract
280 g/10 oz plain flour
1 tbsp cocoa powder
pinch of salt

FILLING
1 egg white
55 g/2 oz caster sugar
85 g/3 oz desiccated coconut
1 tsp plain flour
2 tbsp finely chopped ready-to-eat
    dried papaya

Preheat the oven to 190°C/375°F/Gas Mark 5. Line 2 large baking sheets with baking paper.

To make the middle filling, whisk the egg white in a large bowl until soft peaks form, then gradually whisk in the sugar. Gently fold in the coconut, flour and papaya and reserve.

Place the chocolate in a heatproof bowl, set the bowl over a saucepan of gently simmering water and heat until melted, then remove from the heat. Place the butter and sugar in a large bowl and beat together until light and fluffy, then beat in the egg yolk and vanilla extract. Sift together the flour, cocoa and salt into the mixture and stir until thoroughly combined. Stir in the melted chocolate and knead lightly.

Roll out the dough between 2 sheets of baking paper to 5–8 mm/ ¼–⅜ inch thick. Cut out rounds with a 7-cm/2¾-inch fluted round cutter and place them on the baking sheets. Using a 3-cm/1¼-inch plain round cutter, cut out the centres and remove them. Bake for 8 minutes, then remove from the oven and lower the temperature to 160°C/325°F/ Gas Mark 3. Spoon the filling mixture into the centre of the cookies. Place a sheet of foil over each baking sheet, crumpled so that it doesn't touch the cookies, to stop the filling mixture from browning.

Bake for a further 15–20 minutes, or until the middles are firm. Leave to cool on the baking sheets for 5–10 minutes, then transfer the cookies to wire racks to cool completely.

115 g/4 oz unsalted butter, softened, plus
  extra for greasing
85 g/3 oz demerara sugar
1 tbsp clear honey
115 g/4 oz self-raising flour
pinch of salt
60 g/2¼ oz ready-to-eat dried apricots,
  chopped

50 g/1¾ oz dried figs, chopped
115 g/4 oz porridge oats
1 tsp milk (optional)
40 g/1½ oz sultanas or cranberries
40 g/1½ oz walnut halves, chopped

Preheat the oven to 160°C/325°F/Gas Mark 3. Grease 2 large baking sheets. Place the butter, sugar and honey in a saucepan and heat over a low heat until melted. Mix to combine. Sift together the flour and salt into a large bowl and stir in the apricots, figs and oats. Pour in the butter and sugar mixture and mix to form a dough. If it is too stiff, add a little milk.

Divide the dough into 24 pieces and roll each piece into a ball. Place 12 balls on each baking sheet and press flat to a diameter of 6 cm/2½ inches. Mix the sultanas and walnuts together and press into the cookies. Bake in the preheated oven for 15 minutes, swapping the sheets halfway through. Leave to cool on the baking sheets.

109 *With nutty topping*

Chop 100 g/3½ oz mixed raw nuts and use to top the cookies before baking.

110 *Rather large coconut macaroons*   MAKES 8

2 large egg whites
115 g/4 oz caster sugar
150 g/5½ oz desiccated coconut
8 glacé cherries

Preheat the oven to 180°C/350°F/Gas Mark 4. Line 2–3 large baking sheets with rice paper.

Place the egg whites in a large bowl and whisk until soft peaks form and they hold their shape but are not dry. Add the sugar to the egg whites and, using a large metal spoon, fold in until incorporated. Add the coconut and fold into the mixture. Place 8 heaped tablespoons of the mixture onto the baking sheets and place a cherry on top of each macaroon.

Bake in the preheated oven for 15–20 minutes, or until lightly golden brown around the edges. Leave on the baking sheets for 2–3 minutes, then transfer the macaroons to a wire rack to cool completely.

111 *Nutty macaroons*

Finely chop 50 g/1¾ oz almonds, hazelnuts, macadamia nuts, pecan nuts or walnuts and add to the mixture with the coconut.

225 g/8 oz butter, softened
140 g/5 oz caster sugar
1 egg yolk, lightly beaten
280 g/10 oz plain flour
pinch of salt
½ tsp mixed spice
55 g/2 oz ready-to-eat dried apple,
    finely chopped

½ tsp ground ginger
55 g/2 oz ready-to-eat dried pears,
    finely chopped
25 g/1 oz flaked almonds
1 egg white, lightly beaten
demerara sugar, for sprinkling

Place the butter and sugar in a large bowl and beat together until light and fluffy, then beat in the egg yolk. Sift together the flour and salt into the mixture and stir until combined. Transfer half the dough to another bowl. Add the mixed spice and dried apple to one bowl and mix well. Shape into a ball, wrap in clingfilm and chill for 30–60 minutes.

Add the ginger and dried pear to the other bowl and mix well. Shape into a ball, wrap in clingfilm and chill in the refrigerator for 30–60 minutes.

Preheat the oven to 190°C/375°F/Gas Mark 5. Line 2 large baking sheets with baking paper.

Unwrap the apple-flavoured dough and roll out between 2 sheets of baking paper to about 3 mm/⅛ inch thick. Cut out cookies with a sun-shaped cutter and place them on the baking sheet.

Repeat with the pear-flavoured dough. Cut out cookies with a star-shaped cutter and place them on the other baking sheet.

Bake in the preheated oven for 5 minutes, then remove the star-shaped cookies from the oven and sprinkle with the flaked almonds. Bake for a further 5–10 minutes. Remove the cookies from the oven but do not turn off the heat. Brush the apple suns with a little egg white and sprinkle with demerara sugar, then bake for a further 2–3 minutes. Leave all the cookies to cool for 5–10 minutes, then transfer them onto wire racks to cool completely.

113 *With apple icing*

Replace the flaked almonds, egg white and sugar topping with an apple glacé icing made by sifting 115 g/4 oz icing sugar into a bowl and beating in 1½ tablespoons of apple juice with a drop of green food colouring. Spread onto the cooled cookies.

25 g/1 oz butter, softened, plus extra
    for greasing
15 g/½ oz candied orange peel
25 g/1 oz caster sugar

20 g/¾ oz plain flour
25 g/1 oz ground almonds
finely grated rind of 1 small orange
1 tsp orange juice

Preheat the oven to 180°C/350°F/Gas Mark 4. Grease several large baking sheets. Very finely chop the candied orange peel.

Place the butter and sugar in a large bowl and whisk together until pale and creamy. Add the flour, ground almonds, grated orange rind and juice and mix well together.

Place teaspoonfuls of the mixture onto the baking sheets, spacing them well apart. Bake in the preheated oven for 7–8 minutes, or until lightly golden brown around the edges. Leave on the baking sheets for 2–3 minutes, then transfer the cookies to wire racks to cool completely.

100 g/3½ oz butter, softened, plus extra for greasing
75 g/2¾ oz caster sugar
1 egg, separated
200 g/7 oz plain flour, plus extra for dusting

finely grated rind of 1 orange
finely grated rind of 1 lemon
finely grated rind of 1 lime
2–3 tbsp orange juice

Preheat the oven to 200°C/400°F/Gas Mark 6. Lightly grease 2 large baking sheets. Place the butter and sugar in a large bowl and beat together until light and fluffy, then gradually beat in the egg yolk. Sift the flour into the creamed mixture and mix until thoroughly combined. Add the orange, lemon and lime rinds with enough of the orange juice to form a soft dough.

Roll the dough out on a lightly floured work surface and cut out rounds with a 7.5-cm/3-inch biscuit cutter. Make crescent shapes by cutting away a quarter of each round. Re-roll the trimmings to make about 25 crescents. Place the crescents on the baking sheets and prick the surface of each crescent with a fork. Lightly whisk the egg white in a small bowl and brush it over the biscuits.

Bake in the preheated oven for 12–15 minutes, or until golden brown. Leave the cookies to cool on a wire rack before serving.

116 *With lemon cream*

Make a double quantity of the cookies. Prepare the lemon cream by beating 125 g/4½ oz softened butter with 175 g/6 oz icing sugar and 1 teaspoon of finely grated lemon rind, 1 tablespoon of lemon juice and ½ teaspoon of lemon oil, then use to sandwich the cookies together.

117 *Chocolate temptations*   MAKES 24

90 g/3¼ oz butter, plus extra for greasing
365 g/12½ oz plain chocolate
1 tsp strong coffee
2 eggs
140 g/5 oz soft light brown sugar
185 g/6½ oz plain flour

¼ tsp baking powder
pinch of salt
2 tsp almond extract
85 g/3 oz Brazil nuts, chopped
85 g/3 oz hazelnuts, chopped
40 g/1½ oz white chocolate

Preheat the oven to 180°C/350°F/Gas Mark 4. Grease 2 large baking sheets. Place 225 g/8 oz of the plain chocolate with the butter and coffee into a heatproof bowl, set the bowl over a saucepan of simmering water and heat until the chocolate is almost melted. Remove and stir until smooth.

Beat the eggs in a bowl until fluffy, then gradually whisk in the sugar until thick. Add the chocolate to the egg mixture and stir to combine. Sift the flour, baking powder and salt into a separate bowl and stir into the chocolate. Chop 85 g/3 oz of the plain chocolate into pieces and stir into the mixture. Stir in the almond extract and nuts. Place 24 tablespoonfuls of the mixture onto the baking sheets. Bake in the preheated oven for 16 minutes. Transfer the biscuits to a wire rack to cool. To decorate, melt the remaining plain chocolate and white chocolate, in turn, then spoon into piping bags and pipe lines on the cookies. Leave to set.

118 Rose flower cookies

225 g/8 oz butter, softened
225 g/8 oz caster sugar
1 large egg, lightly beaten
1 tbsp rose water
280 g/10 oz plain flour
1 tsp baking powder
pinch of salt

ICING
1 egg white
250 g/9 oz icing sugar
2 tsp plain flour
2 tsp rose water
few drops of pink food colouring

Place the butter and sugar in a large bowl and beat together until light and fluffy, then beat in the egg and rose water. Sift together the flour, baking powder and salt into the mixture and stir until combined. Shape the dough into a log, wrap in clingfilm and chill in the refrigerator for 1–2 hours.

Preheat the oven to 190°C/375°F/Gas Mark 5. Line 2–3 baking sheets with baking paper.

Unwrap the dough, cut into thin slices with a sharp serrated knife and place on the baking sheets, spaced well apart.

Bake in the preheated oven for 10–12 minutes, or until light golden brown. Leave to cool on the baking sheets for 10 minutes, then transfer the cookies to wire racks to cool completely.

To make the icing, use a fork to lightly beat the egg white in a bowl. Sift in half the icing sugar and stir well, then sift in the remaining icing sugar and flour and mix in enough rose water to make a smooth, easy-to-spread icing. Stir in a few drops of pink food colouring.

Leave the cookies on the racks. Gently spread the icing over them and leave to set.

119 Violet flower cookies

Omit the rose water and pink food colouring. Tint the icing with a little lavender or violet food colouring, then spread the icing on the cookies and scatter over 85 g/3 oz chopped crystallized violets.

120 Zebra cookies

55 g/2 oz plain chocolate, broken into pieces
140 g/5 oz plain flour
1 tsp baking powder
1 egg
140 g/5 oz caster sugar

50 ml/2 fl oz sunflower oil, plus extra for greasing
½ tsp vanilla extract
2 tbsp icing sugar
1 small packet milk chocolate buttons
1 small packet white chocolate buttons

Place the chocolate in a heatproof bowl, set the bowl over a saucepan of gently simmering water and heat until melted. Leave to cool. Sift the flour and baking powder together. Meanwhile, place the egg, sugar, oil and vanilla extract in a large bowl and whisk together. Whisk in the cooled, melted chocolate until well blended, then gradually stir in the sifted flour. Cover the bowl and chill for at least 3 hours.

Preheat the oven to 190°C/375°F/Gas Mark 5. Grease 1–2 large baking sheets with the oil.

Using your hands, shape tablespoonfuls of the mixture into log shapes, each measuring about 5 cm/2 inches. Roll the logs generously in the icing sugar, then place on the baking sheets, spaced well apart. Bake in the preheated oven for 15 minutes, or until firm. As soon as the biscuits are done, place 3 chocolate buttons down the centre of each, alternating the colours. Transfer to a wire rack and leave to cool.

121 With zebra icing

Sift 115 g/4 oz icing sugar into a bowl, add 1 tablespoon of water and mix until smooth. Reserve one quarter and tint with black food colouring. Use the white icing to ice the cookies then add stripes with the black icing and leave to set.

100 g/3½ oz raisins
150 ml/5 fl oz rum
225 g/8 oz butter, softened
140 g/5 oz caster sugar
1 egg yolk, lightly beaten
280 g/10 oz plain flour
pinch of salt

FILLING
175 g/6 oz icing sugar
85 g/3 oz butter, softened
2 tsp finely grated orange rind
1 tsp rum
few drops of yellow food colouring
(optional)

Place the raisins in a bowl, pour in the rum and leave to soak for 15 minutes, then drain, reserving the remaining rum.

Preheat the oven to 190°C/375°F/Gas Mark 5. Line 2 large baking sheets with baking paper.

Place the butter and sugar in a large bowl and beat together until light and fluffy, then beat in the egg yolk and 2 teaspoons of the reserved rum. Sift together the flour and salt into the mixture, add the raisins and stir until thoroughly combined.

Scoop up tablespoons of the dough and place them on the baking sheets, spaced well apart. Flatten gently and smooth the tops with the back of a spoon.

Bake in the preheated oven for 10–15 minutes, or until light golden brown. Leave to cool on the baking sheets for 5–10 minutes, then transfer the cookies to wire racks to cool completely.

To make the orange filling, sift the icing sugar into a bowl, add the butter, orange rind, rum and food colouring, if using, and beat well until smooth. Spread the filling over half the cookies and top with the remaining cookies.

123 With plain chocolate filling

Replace the orange filling with a chocolate filling made by heating 125 ml/4 fl oz double cream to boiling point and pouring over 125 g/4½ oz chopped plain chocolate, then mixing until smooth. Cool and chill until thick, then use to sandwich the biscuits together.

124 Gingernuts

MAKES 30

350 g/12 oz self-raising flour
pinch of salt
200 g/7 oz caster sugar
1 tbsp ground ginger
1 tsp bicarbonate of soda

125 g/4½ oz butter, plus extra
    for greasing
75 g/2¾ oz golden syrup
1 egg, lightly beaten
1 tsp grated orange rind

Preheat the oven to 160°C/325°F/Gas Mark 3. Lightly grease several large baking sheets.

Sift together the flour, salt, sugar, ginger and bicarbonate of soda into a large bowl. Heat the butter and golden syrup together in a saucepan over a very low heat until the butter has melted. Leave to cool slightly, then pour it onto the dry ingredients. Add the egg and orange rind and mix thoroughly to form a dough. Using your hands, carefully shape the dough into 30 even-sized balls.

Place the balls on the baking sheets, spaced well apart, then flatten them slightly with your fingers.

Bake in the preheated oven for 15–20 minutes, then carefully transfer the biscuits to a wire rack to cool.

125 Extra ginger gingernuts

Drain 3 balls of stem ginger in syrup, chop finely and add to the dough before baking.

126 Fennel & angelica cookies

225 g/8 oz butter, softened
140 g/5 oz caster sugar
1 egg yolk, lightly beaten
1 tbsp finely chopped angelica

280 g/10 oz plain flour
pinch of salt
1 tbsp fennel seeds

Place the butter and sugar in a large bowl and beat together until light and fluffy, then beat in the egg yolk and angelica. Sift together the flour and salt into the mixture, add the fennel seeds and stir until thoroughly combined. Shape the dough into a log, wrap in clingfilm and chill in the refrigerator for 30–60 minutes.

Preheat the oven to 190°C/375°F/Gas Mark 5. Line 2 large baking sheets with baking paper. Unwrap the dough, cut into 1-cm/½-inch slices with a sharp serrated knife and place them on the baking sheets, spaced well apart. Bake in the preheated oven for 12–15 minutes, or until golden.

Leave to cool on the baking sheets for 5–10 minutes, then transfer the cookies to wire racks to cool completely.

127 Fennel, lemon & angelica cookies

Add 1 teaspoon of finely grated lemon rind and ½ teaspoon of lemon oil to the dough.

128 Sticky ginger cookies

225 g/8 oz butter, softened
140 g/5 oz caster sugar
1 egg yolk, lightly beaten
55 g/2 oz stem ginger, coarsely chopped,
    plus 1 tbsp syrup from the jar

280 g/10 oz plain flour
pinch of salt
55 g/2 oz plain chocolate chips

Place the butter and sugar in a large bowl and beat together until light and fluffy, then beat in the egg yolk and ginger syrup. Sift together the flour and salt into the mixture, add the stem ginger and chocolate chips and stir until thoroughly combined. Shape the mixture into a log, wrap in clingfilm and chill in the refrigerator for 30–60 minutes.

Preheat the oven to 190°C/375°F/Gas Mark 5. Line 2 large baking sheets with baking paper.

Unwrap the log, cut it into 5-mm/¼-inch slices with a sharp serrated knife and place them on the baking sheets, spaced well apart. Bake in the preheated oven for 12–15 minutes, or until golden brown.

Leave to cool on the baking sheets for 5–10 minutes, then transfer the cookies to wire racks to cool completely.

129 Sticky citrus cookies

Replace the chocolate chips with chopped mixed peel.

200 g/7 oz butter, softened	2 tbsp chopped walnuts
2 tbsp black treacle	pinch of salt
140 g/5 oz caster sugar	
1 egg yolk, lightly beaten	ICING
280 g/10 oz plain flour	115 g/4 oz icing sugar
1 tsp ground cinnamon	1 tbsp hot water
½ tsp grated nutmeg	few drops of yellow food colouring
½ tsp ground cloves	few drops of pink food colouring

Place the butter, treacle and sugar in a large bowl and beat together until fluffy, then beat in the egg yolk.

Sift together the flour, cinnamon, nutmeg, cloves and salt into the mixture, add the walnuts and stir until thoroughly combined. Halve the dough, shape into balls, wrap in clingfilm and chill for 30–60 minutes.

Preheat the oven to 190°C/375°F/Gas Mark 5. Line 2 baking sheets with baking paper. Unwrap the dough and roll out between 2 sheets of baking paper to about 5 mm/¼ inch thick. Cut out rounds with a 6-cm/2½-inch fluted cutter and place them on the baking sheets.

Bake in the preheated oven for 10–15 minutes, or until firm. Leave to cool on the baking sheets for 5–10 minutes, then transfer the cookies to wire racks to cool completely.

To make the icing, sift the icing sugar into a bowl, then gradually stir in the hot water until the icing has the consistency of thick cream. Spoon half the icing into another bowl and stir a few drops of yellow food colouring into one bowl and a few drops of pink food colouring into the other. Leave the cookies on the racks and, using teaspoons, drizzle the yellow icing over them in one direction and the pink icing over them at right angles. Leave to set.

131 *Syrup drizzles*

Replace the treacle with golden syrup and decorate the cookies with the icing leaving out the food colouring.

132 *Cinnamon & orange crisps*

225 g/8 oz butter, softened	4 tsp orange juice
200 g/7 oz caster sugar	280 g/10 oz plain flour
finely grated rind of 1 orange	pinch of salt
1 egg yolk, lightly beaten	2 tsp ground cinnamon

Place the butter, 140 g/5 oz of the sugar and the orange rind in a large bowl and beat together until light and fluffy, then beat in the egg yolk and 2 teaspoons of the orange juice. Sift together the flour and salt into the mixture and stir until thoroughly combined. Shape the dough into a ball, wrap in clingfilm and chill in the refrigerator for 30–60 minutes.

Unwrap the dough and roll out between 2 sheets of baking paper into a 30-cm/12-inch square. Brush with the remaining orange juice and sprinkle with cinnamon. Lightly roll with the rolling pin. Roll up the dough like a Swiss roll. Wrap in clingfilm and chill for 30 minutes.

Preheat the oven to 190°C/375°F/Gas Mark 5. Line 2 large baking sheets with baking paper.

Unwrap the dough and cut into thin slices, then place on the baking sheets, spaced well apart. Bake in the preheated oven for 10–12 minutes. Leave to cool for 5–10 minutes, then transfer to wire racks to cool completely.

133 *With white chocolate coating*

Place 150 g/5½ oz white chocolate in a heatproof bowl, set the bowl over a saucepan of gently simmering water and heat until melted. Dip the cooled cookies to coat half of each one and leave to set on a wire rack.

225 g/8 oz butter, softened
140 g/5 oz caster sugar
1 egg yolk, lightly beaten
2 tsp orange extract
280 g/10 oz plain flour
pinch of salt

100 g/3½ oz plain chocolate chips

CINNAMON COATING
1½ tbsp caster sugar
1½ tbsp ground cinnamon

Preheat the oven to 190°C/375°F/Gas Mark 5. Line 2 large baking sheets with baking paper. Place the butter and sugar in a large bowl and beat together until light and fluffy, then beat in the egg yolk and orange extract. Sift together the flour and salt into the mixture, add the chocolate chips and stir until thoroughly combined.

To make the cinnamon coating, mix the sugar and cinnamon together in a shallow dish. Scoop out tablespoons of the cookie dough, roll them into balls, then roll them in the cinnamon mixture to coat. Place them on the baking sheets, spaced well apart.

Bake in the preheated oven for 12–15 minutes, or until golden brown. Leave to cool on the baking sheets for 5–10 minutes, then transfer the cookies to wire racks to cool completely.

135 *White chocolate & spice cookies*

Replace the plain chocolate chips with 100 g/3½ oz white chocolate chips and replace the cinnamon with 1 tablespoon of ground mixed spice and ½ teaspoon of ground nutmeg.

136 *Papaya & cashew nut cookies* MAKES ABOUT 30

225 g/8 oz butter, softened
140 g/5 oz caster sugar
1 egg yolk, lightly beaten
2 tsp lime juice
280 g/10 oz plain flour

pinch of salt
100 g/3½ oz ready-to-eat dried papaya, chopped
100 g/3 oz cashew nuts, finely chopped

Place the butter and sugar in a large bowl and beat together until light and fluffy, then beat in the egg yolk and lime juice.

Sift together the flour and salt into the mixture, add the papaya and stir until thoroughly combined.

Spread out the cashew nuts in a shallow dish. Shape the dough into a log and roll in the nuts to coat. Wrap the dough in clingfilm and chill in the refrigerator for 30–60 minutes.

Preheat the oven to 190°C/375°F/Gas Mark 5. Line 2 large baking sheets with baking paper.

Unwrap the dough, cut into slices with a sharp serrated knife and place them on the baking sheets, spaced well apart.

Bake in the preheated oven for 12–15 minutes, or until light golden. Leave to cool on the baking sheets for 5–10 minutes, then transfer the cookies to wire racks to cool completely.

137 *With cashew icing*

Beat 85 g/3 oz unsalted butter, 100 g/3½ oz icing sugar and 100 g/3½ oz cashew nut butter together until smooth and spread over the cooled cookies.

138 *Peach daiquiri cookies*

225 g/8 oz butter, softened
140 g/5 oz caster sugar
finely grated rind of 1 lime
1 egg yolk, lightly beaten
2 tsp white rum
280 g/10 oz plain flour
pinch of salt

100 g/3½ oz ready-to-eat dried peaches,
   chopped

ICING
140 g/5 oz icing sugar
2 tbsp white rum

Preheat the oven to 190°C/375°F/ Gas Mark 5. Line 2 baking sheets with baking paper.

Place the butter, sugar and lime rind in a large bowl and beat together until light and fluffy, then beat in the egg yolk and rum. Sift together the flour and salt into the mixture, add the peaches and stir until thoroughly combined. Scoop up tablespoons of the dough and place them on the baking sheets, then flatten gently. Bake in the preheated oven for 10–15 minutes, or until light golden brown. Leave to cool on the baking sheets for 5–10 minutes, then transfer the cookies to wire racks to cool completely.

Sift the icing sugar into a bowl and stir in enough rum until the mixture is the consistency of thick cream. Leave the cookies on the wire racks and drizzle the icing over them with a teaspoon. Leave to set.

139 *With peach icing*

Omit the dried peaches from the cookie dough and instead stir them into a double quantity of icing. Spoon the icing onto the cooled cookies, then spread to cover and leave to set.

140 *Peach, pear & plum cookies*

225 g/8 oz butter, softened
140 g/5 oz caster sugar
1 egg yolk, lightly beaten
2 tsp almond extract
280 g/10 oz plain flour
pinch of salt

55 g/2 oz ready-to-eat dried peaches,
   finely chopped
55 g/2 oz ready-to-eat dried pears, finely
   chopped
4 tbsp plum jam

Preheat the oven to 190°C/375°F/Gas Mark 5. Line 2 large baking sheets with baking paper. Place the butter and sugar in a large bowl and beat together until light and fluffy, then beat in the egg yolk and almond extract. Sift together the flour and salt into the mixture, add the dried fruit and stir until thoroughly combined.

Scoop up tablespoons of the mixture, roll them into balls and place on the baking sheets, spaced well apart. Make a hollow in the centre of each with the dampened handle of a wooden spoon and fill the hollows with the jam. Bake in the preheated oven for 12–15 minutes, or until light golden brown.

Leave to cool on the baking sheets for 5–10 minutes, then transfer the cookies to wire racks to cool completely.

141 *Extra peachy cookies*

Replace the plum jam with peach preserve and serve topped with chopped fresh peach.

150 g/5½ oz unsalted butter, softened
50 g/1¾ oz icing sugar
½ tsp vanilla extract

150 g/5½ oz plain flour
pinch of salt
70 g/2½ oz glacé cherries, finely chopped

Preheat the oven to 190°C/375°F/Gas Mark 5. Place the butter and sugar in a large bowl and beat together until light and fluffy. Add the vanilla extract and beat until combined. Sift in the flour and salt in batches, mixing well between each addition. Add the cherries and mix well.

Spoon the mixture into a piping bag fitted with a 2.5-cm/1-inch star nozzle and pipe rings onto 2 large non-stick baking sheets. Bake in the preheated oven for 8–10 minutes, or until light golden. Leave to cool on a wire rack.

143 *With cherry icing*

Make a butter icing with 85 g/3oz unsalted butter beaten with 150 g/5½ oz icing sugar and adding 50 g/1¾ oz chopped glacé cherries. Pipe the icing onto the cookies and decorate with small pieces of angelica.

144 *Pistachio & almond cookies* 　MAKES ABOUT 30

225 g/8 oz butter, softened
140 g/5 oz caster sugar
1 egg yolk, lightly beaten
2 tsp almond extract

225 g/8 oz plain flour
pinch of salt
55 g/2 oz ground almonds
55 g/2 oz pistachio nuts, finely chopped

Place the butter and sugar in a large bowl and beat together until light and fluffy, then beat in the egg yolk and almond extract. Sift together the flour and salt into the mixture, add the ground almonds and stir until thoroughly combined. Halve the dough, shape into balls, wrap in clingfilm and chill in the refrigerator for 30–60 minutes.

Preheat the oven to 190°C/375°F/Gas Mark 5. Line 2 large baking sheets with baking paper. Unwrap the dough and roll out between 2 sheets of baking paper to about 3 mm/⅛ inch thick. Sprinkle half the pistachio nuts over each piece of dough and roll lightly with the rolling pin. Cut out cookies with a heart-shaped cutter and place them on the baking sheets, spaced well apart.

Bake in the preheated oven for 10–12 minutes. Leave to cool for 5–10 minutes, then transfer the cookies to wire racks to cool completely.

145 *With pistachio cream*

Whisk 200 ml/7 fl oz double cream to soft peaks with 2 tablespoons of icing sugar and ½ teaspoon of green food colouring. Fold in 85 g/3 oz chopped shelled pistachios and spoon into a bowl, then use as a dip for the cookies.

115 g/4 oz butter, softened
125 g/4½ oz caster sugar
125 g/4½ oz soft light brown sugar
2 large eggs, lightly beaten
1 tsp vanilla extract
280 g/10 oz plain flour
1 tsp bicarbonate of soda
300 g/10½ oz chocolate chunks

Preheat the oven to 180°C/350°F/ Gas Mark 4. Line several large baking sheets with baking paper.

Place the butter and sugars in a large bowl and whisk together until pale and creamy. Whisk the eggs and vanilla extract into the mixture until smooth. Sift in the flour and bicarbonate of soda and beat together until well mixed. Stir in the chocolate chunks.

Drop 12 large spoonfuls of the mixture onto the baking sheets, spacing them well apart.

Bake in the preheated oven for 15–20 minutes, or until set and golden brown. Leave to cool on the baking sheets for 2–3 minutes, then transfer the cookies to a wire rack and leave to cool completely.

147 *Giant chocolate chip cookies*

Replace the chocolate chunks with chocolate chips. These can be plain, milk or white chocolate, or use some of each.

148 *Indulgent chocolate chunk cookies*

Scatter 100 g/3½ oz chocolate chunks over the top of the cookies before baking in the oven.

149 Camomile cookies

225 g/8 oz butter, softened
140 g/5 oz caster sugar, plus extra for
    coating
1 tbsp (3–4 tea bags) camomile or
    camomile and lime flower infusion tea
1 egg yolk, lightly beaten

1 tsp vanilla extract
280 g/10 oz plain flour
pinch of salt

Place the butter and sugar in a large bowl and beat together until light
and fluffy. If using tea bags, remove the tea leaves from the bags. Stir the
tea into the butter mixture, then beat in the egg yolk and vanilla extract.
Sift together the flour and salt into the mixture and stir until thoroughly
combined. Shape the dough into a log. Spread out the extra sugar in a
shallow dish and roll the log in the sugar to coat. Wrap in clingfilm and
chill in the refrigerator for 30–60 minutes.

Preheat the oven to 190°C/375°F/Gas Mark 5. Line 2 large baking
sheets with baking paper.

Unwrap the log, cut into 5-mm/¼-inch slices with a sharp serrated
knife and place them on the baking sheets, spaced well apart. Bake in
the preheated oven for 10 minutes, or until golden. Leave to cool on the
baking sheets for 5–10 minutes, then transfer the cookies to wire racks
to cool completely.

150 Lemon verbena cookies

*Replace the camomile tea with lemon verbena tea and add ½ teaspoon
of finely grated lemon rind to the dough.*

151 Nutty pecan cookies

150 g/5½ oz unsalted butter, softened
150 g/5½ oz caster sugar
225 g/8 oz self-raising flour

1–2 tbsp milk
½ tsp vanilla extract
280 g/10 oz pecan nuts

Preheat the oven to 190°C/375°F/Gas Mark 5. Line 2 large baking sheets
with baking paper. Place the butter and sugar in a large bowl and beat
together until light and fluffy. Sift in the flour and beat to combine. Add
1 tablespoon of milk and the vanilla extract and mix to form a dough,
adding more milk if the dough is too stiff.

Reserve 20 pecan halves. Chop the remaining pecan nuts and knead
in to the dough. Divide the dough into 20 and roll each piece into a ball.
Place 10 balls on each baking sheet, spaced well apart. Press down to a
thickness of 1 cm/½ inch, then press a pecan half into the centre of each
cookie. Bake in the preheated oven for 10–15 minutes. Leave the cookies
to cool on the baking sheets.

152 *Cappuccino cookies*

2 sachets instant cappuccino
1 tbsp hot water
225 g/8 oz butter, softened
140 g/5 oz caster sugar
1 egg yolk, lightly beaten
280 g/10 oz plain flour

pinch of salt

TOPPING
175 g/6 oz white chocolate, broken
   into pieces
cocoa powder, for dusting

Empty the cappuccino sachets into a small bowl and stir in the hot, but not boiling, water to make a paste. Place the butter and sugar in a large bowl and beat together until light and fluffy, then beat in the egg yolk and cappuccino paste. Sift together the flour and salt into the mixture and stir until combined. Halve the dough, shape into balls, wrap in clingfilm and chill for 30–60 minutes.

Preheat the oven to 190°C/375°F/Gas Mark 5. Line 2 large baking sheets with baking paper. Then unwrap the dough and roll it out between 2 sheets of baking paper. Cut out cookies with a 6-cm/2½-inch round cutter and place them on the baking sheets, spaced well apart. Bake in the preheated oven for 10–12 minutes, or until golden brown. Leave to cool for 5–10 minutes, then transfer to wire racks to cool completely.

Place the wire racks over a sheet of baking paper. Place the chocolate into a heatproof bowl, set the bowl over a saucepan of gently simmering water and heat until melted. Leave to cool, then spoon the chocolate over the cookies. Leave to set, then dust lightly with cocoa powder.

153 *With coffee bean topping*

Replace the cocoa powder with 100 g/3½ oz crushed chocolate-covered coffee beans, scatter them over the melted white chocolate topping and leave to set.

154 *Cinnamon & caramel cookies*

225 g/8 oz butter, softened
140 g/5 oz caster sugar
1 egg yolk, lightly beaten
1 tsp vanilla extract
280 g/10 oz plain flour

1 tsp ground cinnamon
½ tsp allspice
pinch of salt
25–30 caramels

Preheat the oven to 190°C/375°F/Gas Mark 5. Line 2 large baking sheets with baking paper. Place the butter and sugar in a large bowl and beat together until light and fluffy, then beat in the egg yolk and vanilla extract. Sift together the flour, cinnamon, allspice and salt into the mixture and stir until thoroughly combined.

Scoop up tablespoons of the mixture, shape into balls and place on the baking sheets, spaced well apart. Bake in the preheated oven for 8 minutes. Place a caramel on top of each cookie and bake for a further 6–7 minutes. Leave to cool on the baking sheets for 5–10 minutes, then transfer to wire racks to cool completely.

155 *Lemon & sweetie cookies*

Replace the cinnamon and allspice with 1 teaspoon of finely grated lemon rind. Replace the caramels with 25 lemon boiled sweets.

156 Almond crunchies

225 g/8 oz butter, softened
140 g/5 oz caster sugar
1 egg yolk, lightly beaten
½ tsp almond extract

225 g/8 oz plain flour
pinch of salt
225 g/8 oz blanched almonds, chopped

Place the butter and sugar in a large bowl and beat together until light and fluffy, then beat in the egg yolk and almond extract. Sift together the flour and salt into the mixture, add the almonds and stir until thoroughly combined. Halve the dough, shape it into balls, wrap in clingfilm and chill in the refrigerator for 30–60 minutes.

Preheat the oven to 190°C/375°F/Gas Mark 5. Line 2–3 baking sheets with baking paper.

Shape the dough into about 50 small balls, flatten them slightly between the palms of your hands and place them on the baking sheets, spaced well apart. Bake in the preheated oven for 15–20 minutes, or until golden brown. Leave to cool on the baking sheets for 5–10 minutes, then transfer to wire racks to cool completely.

157 With marzipan filling

Cut 100 g/3½ oz marzipan into small cubes and press one piece into the middle of each cookie. Form the dough around the marzipan to completely enclose and bake as before.

158 Almond & raspberry jam drops

225 g/8 oz butter, softened
140 g/5 oz caster sugar
1 egg yolk, lightly beaten
2 tsp almond extract
280 g/10 oz plain flour

pinch of salt
55 g/2 oz almonds, toasted and chopped
55 g/2 oz chopped mixed peel
4 tbsp raspberry jam

Preheat the oven to 190°C/375°F/Gas Mark 5. Line 2 baking sheets with baking paper. Place the butter and sugar in a large bowl and beat together until light and fluffy, then beat in the egg yolk and almond extract. Sift together the flour and salt into the mixture, add the almonds and mixed peel and stir until thoroughly combined.

Scoop out tablespoons of the mixture and shape into balls with your hands, then place them on the baking sheets, spaced well apart. Use the dampened handle of a wooden spoon to make a hollow in the centre of each cookie and fill with raspberry jam. Bake in the preheated oven for 12–15 minutes, or until golden brown. Leave to cool for 5–10 minutes, then transfer to wire racks to cool completely.

159 Almond & strawberry jam drops

Replace the mixed peel with 55 g/2 oz chopped dried strawberries and replace the raspberry jam with strawberry jam.

200 g/7 oz butter, plus extra for greasing
275 g/9¾ oz demerara sugar
1 egg
140 g/5 oz plain flour
1 tsp baking powder
1 tsp bicarbonate of soda
125 g/4½ oz rolled oats
1 tbsp bran
1 tbsp wheatgerm
115 g/4 oz mixed nuts, toasted and roughly chopped
200 g/7 oz plain chocolate chips
115 g/4 oz mixed raisins and sultanas
175 g/6 oz plain chocolate, roughly chopped

Preheat the oven to 180°C/350°F/Gas Mark 4. Grease 2 large baking sheets. Place the butter, sugar and egg in a large bowl and beat together until light and fluffy. Sift in the flour, baking powder and bicarbonate of soda. Add the oats, bran and wheatgerm and mix together until well combined. Stir in the nuts, chocolate chips and dried fruit. Place 24 rounded tablespoons of the mixture on the baking sheets.

Bake in the preheated oven for 12 minutes, or until golden brown. Leave to cool on wire racks.

Meanwhile, place the chocolate pieces in a heatproof bowl, set the bowl over a saucepan of gently simmering water and heat until melted. Stir the chocolate, then leave to cool slightly. Use a spoon to drizzle the chocolate in waves over the cookies, or spoon it into a piping bag and pipe zigzag lines over the biscuits.

161 *With nut chocolate topping*

Add 115 g/4 oz chopped mixed nuts to the melted chocolate and spread over the cookies.

162 *Cashew & poppy seed cookies*

225 g/8 oz butter, softened
140 g/5 oz caster sugar
1 egg yolk, lightly beaten
280 g/10 oz plain flour
1 tsp ground cinnamon
pinch of salt
115 g/4 oz cashew nuts, chopped
2–3 tbsp poppy seeds

Place the butter and sugar in a large bowl and beat together until light and fluffy, then beat in the egg yolk. Sift together the flour, cinnamon and salt into the mixture, add the nuts and stir until combined. Shape the dough into a log. Spread out the poppy seeds in a dish and roll the log in them until coated. Wrap in clingfilm and chill for 30–60 minutes.

Preheat the oven to 190°C/375°F/Gas Mark 5. Line 2 large baking sheets with baking paper.

Unwrap the dough, cut into 1-cm/½-inch slices with a sharp serrated knife and place them on the baking sheets. Bake in the preheated oven for 12 minutes, or until golden brown. Leave to cool on the baking sheets for 5–10 minutes, then transfer to wire racks to cool completely.

163 *Cashew cookies*

Omit the poppy seeds and roll the dough in 225 g/8 oz finely chopped cashew nuts.

175 g/6 oz butter, plus extra for greasing
200 g/7 oz soft light brown sugar
1 egg
70 g/2½ oz plain flour, plus extra for
    dusting (optional)
1 tsp bicarbonate of soda
pinch of salt
70 g/2½ oz wholemeal flour

1 tbsp bran
225 g/8 oz plain chocolate chips
185 g/6½ oz rolled oats
1 tbsp strong coffee
100 g/3½ oz hazelnuts, toasted
    and roughly chopped

Preheat the oven to 190°C/375°F/Gas Mark 5. Grease 2 large baking sheets. Place the butter and sugar in a large bowl and beat together until light and fluffy. Add the egg and beat well. Sift together the plain flour, bicarbonate of soda and salt into another bowl, then add in the wholemeal flour and bran. Mix in the egg mixture, then stir in the chocolate chips, oats, coffee and hazelnuts and mix well.

Place 24 rounded tablespoons of the mixture on the baking sheets, spaced well apart. Alternatively, with lightly floured hands, break off pieces of the mixture and roll into balls (about 25 g/1 oz each), place on the baking sheets and flatten.

Bake in the preheated oven for 16–18 minutes, or until golden brown. Leave to cool for 5 minutes, then transfer to a wire rack to cool completely.

165 *With ice cream filling*

Remove a tub of plain chocolate ice cream from the freezer and leave to soften at room temperature. Tip into a bowl and add 2 tablespoons of Kahlúa coffee liqueur and beat together. Use to sandwich the baked cookies together, then freeze the cookies for 10 minutes until firm. Makes 12.

166 *Jumbo oat & raisin chippers*   MAKES 15

85 g/3 oz rolled oats
100 g/3½ oz plain flour
½ tsp bicarbonate of soda
pinch of salt
60 g/2¼ oz unsalted butter, softened

100 g/3½ oz soft light brown sugar
50 g/1¾ oz granulated sugar
1 large egg
½ tsp vanilla extract
175 g/6 oz raisins

Preheat the oven to 190°C/375°F/Gas Mark 5. Place the oats in a food processor and pulse briefly, then tip into a bowl and sift in the flour, bicarbonate of soda and salt and stir together.

Place the butter and sugars in a large bowl and beat together until light and fluffy. Place the egg and vanilla extract in a separate bowl and whisk together, then add to the butter and mix well. Add the flour mixture, mix together, then add the raisins and mix thoroughly.

Divide the mixture into 15 balls and place on 2 large non-stick baking sheets, spaced well apart. Press the cookies into rough rounds. Bake in the preheated oven for 12 minutes, or until golden brown. Leave to cool for 5 minutes, then transfer to a wire rack to cool completely.

167 *Jumbo oat, apricot & prune chippers*

Replace the raisins with 100 g/3½ oz chopped dried apricots and 100 g/ 3½ oz chopped pitted prunes.

115 g/4 oz butter, softened, plus extra
   for greasing
115 g/4 oz light muscovado sugar
85 g/3 oz caster sugar
1 tsp vanilla extract
1 tbsp instant coffee granules, dissolved in
   1 tbsp hot water

1 egg
175 g/6 oz plain flour
½ tsp baking powder
¼ tsp bicarbonate of soda
55 g/2 oz milk chocolate chips
55 g/2 oz walnut halves, roughly chopped

Preheat the oven to 180°C/350°F/Gas Mark 4. Grease 2 large baking sheets. Place the butter and sugars in a large bowl and beat together until light and fluffy. Place the vanilla extract, coffee and egg in a separate bowl and whisk together. Gradually add the coffee mixture to the butter and sugar, beating until fluffy. Sift the flour, baking powder and bicarbonate of soda into the mixture and fold in carefully. Fold in the chocolate chips and walnuts.

Spoon heaped teaspoons of the mixture onto the baking sheets, spaced well apart. Bake in the preheated oven for 10–15 minutes, or until crisp on the outside but soft inside. Leave to cool on the baking sheets for 2 minutes, then transfer to wire racks to cool completely

169 *With mocha icing*

Sift 100 g/3½ oz icing sugar into a bowl. Stir ½ teaspoon of instant espresso powder, ½ teaspoon of cocoa powder and 1 tablespoon of boiling water together until smooth. Add to the icing sugar and mix to a smooth icing, spread over the cookies and leave to set on a wire rack.

170 *Almond tuilles*

1 tsp groundnut oil, for greasing
85 g/3 oz unsalted butter, softened
70 g/2½ oz caster sugar

50 g/1¾ oz plain flour
pinch of salt
70 g/2½ oz flaked almonds

Preheat the oven to 200°C/400°F/Gas Mark 6 and grease 2 large baking sheets with the oil. Place the butter and sugar in a large bowl and beat together until light and fluffy. Sift together the flour and salt and fold into the mixture, then add the almonds and mix together.

Drop 12 teaspoons of batter on each baking sheet, spaced well apart, and spread into flat ovals with the back of a spoon.

Bake in the preheated oven for 5 minutes, or until golden. While the cookies are still warm, lift each one in turn and drape over a wooden rolling pin to make a curved shape. Leave for 1 minute to harden, then transfer to a wire rack to cool completely.

171 *With chocolate coating*

Place 150 g/5½ oz plain chocolate in a heatproof bowl, set the bowl over a saucepan of gently simmering water and heat until melted. Dip each tuille into the melted chocolate and leave to set on baking paper.

½ tsp groundnut oil, for greasing
225 g/8 oz unsalted butter, softened
200 g/7 oz granulated sugar
1 tsp vanilla extract
280 g/10 oz plain flour

pinch of salt
175 g/6 oz milk chocolate chips
150 g/5½ oz pecan nuts, chopped
150 g/5½ oz almonds, toasted
   and chopped

Preheat the oven to 190°C/375°F/Gas Mark 5. Grease a 38 x 25-cm/ 15 x 10-inch Swiss roll tin with the oil. Place the butter and sugar in a large bowl and beat together until light and fluffy, then stir in the vanilla extract. Sift together the flour and salt into the mixture and beat until combined. Mix in 90 g/3¼ oz of the chocolate chips and the nuts and press the mixture into the tin, making sure the dough fills the tin and is evenly spread. Bake in the preheated oven for 20–25 minutes, or until golden. Leave to cool in the tin.

Place the remaining chocolate chips in a heatproof bowl, set the bowl over a saucepan of gently simmering water and heat until melted. Drizzle the chocolate over the cookie brittle and leave to set, then break the brittle into irregular pieces.

173   *Lemon almond brittle*

Omit the chocolate and nuts, and add the finely grated rind of 2 lemons to the mixture before pressing into the tin. Top with 150 g/5½ oz flaked almonds and bake as before. Cool and break into pieces.

174   *Dark & white chocolate cookies*   MAKES ABOUT 24

200 g/7 oz butter, softened, plus extra
   for greasing
200 g/7 oz caster sugar
½ tsp vanilla extract
1 large egg

225 g/8 oz plain flour
pinch of salt
1 tsp bicarbonate of soda
115 g/4 oz white chocolate chips
115 g/4 oz plain chocolate chips

Preheat the oven to 180°C/350°F/Gas Mark 4. Grease 2 large baking sheets. Place the butter, sugar and vanilla extract in a large bowl and beat together. Gradually beat in the egg until the mixture is light and fluffy. Sift the flour, salt and bicarbonate of soda over the mixture and fold in. Fold in the chocolate chips.

Drop heaped teaspoonfuls of the mixture onto the baking sheets, spaced well apart. Bake in the preheated oven for 10–12 minutes, or until crisp outside but still soft inside.

Leave to cool on the baking sheets for 2 minutes, then transfer the cookies to wire racks to cool completely.

175   *Dark chocolate & hazelnut cookies*

Replace the white chocolate chips with chopped toasted hazelnuts.

176 Ice cream cookie sandwiches

225 g/8 oz butter, softened
140 g/5 oz caster sugar
1 egg yolk, lightly beaten
2 tbsp finely chopped stem ginger, plus
    2 tsp syrup from the jar
250 g/9 oz plain flour

25 g/1 oz cocoa powder
½ tsp ground cinnamon
pinch of salt
450 ml/15 fl oz vanilla, chocolate
    or coffee ice cream

Place the butter and sugar in a large bowl and beat together until light and fluffy, then beat in the egg yolk, ginger and ginger syrup. Sift together the flour, cocoa powder, cinnamon and salt into the mixture and stir until combined. Halve the dough, shape into balls, wrap in clingfilm and chill for 30–60 minutes.

Preheat the oven to 190°C/375°F/Gas Mark 5. Line 2 large baking sheets with baking paper. Unwrap the dough and roll out between 2 sheets of baking paper. Cut out cookies with a 6-cm/2½-inch fluted round cutter and place them on the baking sheets, spaced well apart.

Bake in the preheated oven for 10–15 minutes, or until light golden brown. Leave to cool for 5–10 minutes, then transfer to wire racks to cool completely.

Remove the ice cream from the freezer about 15 minutes before serving, to allow it to soften. Put a generous scoop of ice cream on half the cookies and top with the remaining cookies. Press together gently so that the filling spreads to the edges. If not serving immediately, wrap the cookies individually in foil and store in the freezer.

177 Chocolate mint sandwiches

Replace the stem ginger in the cookie dough with 1 teaspoon of peppermint extract, then fill the cookies with chocolate chip ice cream.

178 Coffee cream & walnut cookies

225 g/8 oz butter, softened
140 g/5 oz caster sugar
1 egg yolk, lightly beaten
2 tsp vanilla extract
225 g/8 oz plain flour
pinch of salt
55 g/2 oz ground walnuts
55 g/2 oz walnuts, finely chopped
icing sugar, for dusting (optional)

COFFEE CREAM
85 g/3 oz butter, softened
140 g/5 oz icing sugar
1½ tsp strong black coffee

Place the butter and sugar in a large bowl and beat together until light and fluffy, then beat in the egg yolk and vanilla extract. Sift together the flour and salt into the mixture, add the ground walnuts and stir until combined. Halve the dough, shape into balls, wrap in clingfilm and chill in the refrigerator for 30–60 minutes.

Preheat the oven to 190°C/375°F/Gas Mark 5. Line 2 baking sheets with baking paper. Unwrap the dough and roll out between 2 sheets of baking paper. Cut out cookies with a 6-cm/2½-inch fluted round cutter and place them on the baking sheets, spaced well apart.

Bake in the preheated oven for 10–15 minutes, or until light golden brown. Leave to cool on the baking sheets for 5–10 minutes, then transfer the cookies to wire racks to cool completely.

To make the coffee cream, place the butter and icing sugar in a bowl and beat together until smooth and thoroughly combined, then beat in the coffee.

Sandwich the cookies together in pairs with the coffee cream, then press together gently so that the cream oozes out of the sides. Smooth the sides with a dampened finger. Spread out the chopped walnuts in a shallow dish and roll the cookies in them to coat the sides of the coffee cream filling. Dust the tops with sifted icing sugar, if liked.

179 Chocolate cream & walnut cookies

Replace the coffee with 1 teaspoon of cocoa powder.

115 g/4 oz unsalted butter, softened
250 g/9 oz light soft brown sugar
1 large egg, lightly beaten
2 tsp vanilla extract
275 g/9½ oz plain flour
15 g/½ oz cocoa powder
1 tsp bicarbonate of soda
1 tsp salt
200 g/7 oz plain chocolate, chopped
150 g/5½ oz milk chocolate, chopped

Preheat the oven to 180°C/350°F/Gas Mark 4. Line 2 large baking sheets with non-stick baking paper. Place the butter and sugar in a large bowl and beat together until light and fluffy. Place the egg and vanilla extract in a separate bowl and whisk together, then gradually add to the butter mixture and beat until smooth. Mix in the flour, cocoa powder, bicarbonate of soda and salt until well combined. Add 100 g/3½ oz each of the plain and milk chocolates, then mix well.

Spoon 6 heaped tablespoons of the mixture onto each baking sheet, spacing them well apart. Divide the remaining chocolate among the cookies and press in lightly.

Bake in the preheated oven for 15–17 minutes. Leave to cool on the baking sheets for 5 minutes, then transfer to a wire rack to cool.

181 *With extra chocolate*

Place 150 g/5½ oz milk chocolate in a heatproof bowl, set the bowl over a saucepan of gently simmering water and heat until melted. Leave to cool for a few minutes then spread over the cold cookies and leave to set.

182 *Peanut butter cookies*   MAKES ABOUT 26

115 g/4 oz butter, softened, plus extra
    for greasing
115 g/4 oz crunchy peanut butter
115 g/4 oz golden caster sugar
115 g/4 oz light muscovado sugar
1 egg, lightly beaten
½ tsp vanilla extract
85 g/3 oz plain flour
½ tsp bicarbonate of soda
½ tsp baking powder
pinch of salt
115 g/4 oz rolled oats

Preheat the oven to 180°C/350°F/Gas Mark 4. Grease 3 large baking sheets. Place the butter and peanut butter in a bowl and beat together, then beat in the sugars. Gradually beat in the egg and vanilla extract. Sift the flour, bicarbonate of soda, baking powder and salt into the mixture, add the oats and stir until just combined.

Place spoonfuls of the mixture on the baking sheets, spaced well apart, and flatten slightly with a fork. Bake in the preheated oven for 12 minutes, or until lightly browned. Leave to cool on the baking sheets for 2 minutes, then transfer to wire racks to cool completely.

183 *With banana filling*

Spread a cookie with smooth peanut butter and top with thin slices of banana tossed in lemon juice, then top with a second cookie and sandwich together. Makes about 13.

Carrot cake cookies

115 g/4 oz butter, softened
85 g/3 oz caster sugar
75 g/2¾ oz soft light brown sugar
1 large egg
½ tsp vanilla extract
150 g/5½ oz plain flour

½ tsp bicarbonate of soda
½ tsp ground cinnamon
25 g/1 oz desiccated coconut
85 g/3 oz carrots, finely grated
25 g/1 oz walnut halves, chopped

Preheat the oven to 190°C/375°F/Gas Mark 5. Line several large baking sheets with baking paper.

Place the butter and sugars in a large bowl and whisk together until pale and creamy. Whisk the egg and vanilla extract into the mixture until smooth. Sift in the flour, bicarbonate of soda and cinnamon, then beat together until well mixed. Add the grated carrot, chopped walnuts and coconut to the mixture and mix well together.

Drop heaped teaspoonfuls of the mixture onto the baking sheets, spaced well apart. Bake in the preheated oven for 8–10 minutes, or until lightly golden brown around the edges.

Leave to cool on the baking sheets for 2–3 minutes, then transfer to a wire rack to cool completely.

185 *Frosted carrot cake cookies*

When the cookies are cold, top with a cream cheese frosting. Put 40 g/ 1½ oz soft cream cheese, 25 g/1 oz butter and ½ teaspoon of vanilla extract in a large bowl and beat together until smooth. Sift in 200 g/7 oz icing sugar and beat together until combined, then spread on top of the cookies.

186 *Banana & chocolate cookies*

125 g/4½ oz butter
125 g/4½ oz caster sugar
1 large egg, lightly beaten
1 ripe banana, mashed
175 g/6 oz self-raising flour

1 tsp mixed spice
2 tbsp milk
100 g/3½ oz chocolate, cut into chunks
55 g/2 oz raisins

Preheat the oven to 190°C/375°F/Gas Mark 5. Line 2 large baking sheets with baking paper. Place the butter and sugar in a large bowl and beat together until light and fluffy. Gradually add the egg, beating well after each addition. Mash the banana and add it to the mixture, beating well until smooth.

Sift together the flour and mixed spice into the mixture and fold in with a spatula. Add the milk to give a soft consistency, then fold in the chocolate and raisins. Drop dessertspoons of the mixture onto the baking sheets, spaced well apart. Bake in the centre of the preheated oven for 15–20 minutes, or until lightly golden. Leave to cool slightly, then transfer to a wire rack to cool completely.

187 *Pistachio biscotti*

225 g/8 oz butter, softened
140 g/5 oz caster sugar
finely grated rind of 1 lemon
1 egg yolk, lightly beaten
2 tsp brandy

280 g/10 oz plain flour
85 g/3 oz pistachio nuts
pinch of salt
icing sugar, for dusting

Place the butter, sugar and lemon rind in a large bowl and beat together until light and fluffy, then beat in the egg yolk and brandy. Sift together the flour, pistachio nuts and salt into the mixture and stir until thoroughly combined. Shape the mixture into a log, flatten slightly, wrap in clingfilm and chill in the refrigerator for 30–60 minutes.

Preheat the oven to 190°C/375°F/Gas Mark 5. Line 2 large baking sheets with baking paper. Unwrap the log, cut it slightly on the diagonal into 5-mm/¼-inch slices with a sharp serrated knife and place them on the baking sheets.

Bake in the oven for 10 minutes, or until golden brown. Leave to cool for 5–10 minutes, then transfer to wire racks to cool completely. Dust with sifted icing sugar.

188 *Hazelnut biscotti*

Replace the pistachio nuts with hazelnuts and replace the lemon rind with the finely grated rind of 1 orange.

189 *Zesty lemon biscotti*

butter, for greasing
280 g/10 oz plain flour, plus extra
    for dusting
1 tsp baking powder

150 g/5½ oz caster sugar
85 g/3 oz blanched almonds
2 large eggs, lightly beaten
finely grated rind and juice of 1 lemon

Preheat the oven to 180°C/350°F/Gas Mark 4. Grease a large baking sheet. Sift the flour and baking powder into a large bowl. Add the sugar, almonds, beaten eggs, lemon rind and juice to the flour and mix together to form a soft dough. Turn the dough onto a lightly floured work surface and, with floured hands, knead for 2–3 minutes, or until smooth.

Divide the dough in half and shape each portion into a log shape measuring about 4 cm/1½ inches in diameter. Place the logs on the baking sheet and flatten until each is about 2.5 cm/1 inch thick.

Bake in the preheated oven for 25 minutes, or until lightly golden brown. Remove from the oven. Reduce the oven temperature to 150°C/300°F/Gas Mark 2. Leave to cool for 15 minutes.

Using a serrated knife, cut the baked dough into 1-cm/½-inch thick slices and place cut-side down on ungreased baking sheets. Bake for a further 10 minutes. Turn and bake for 10–15 minutes, or until golden brown and crisp. Transfer to a wire rack and leave to cool and harden.

190 *Zesty orange & walnut biscotti*

Replace the grated lemon rind and juice with orange. Replace the almonds with chopped walnut halves.

191 Almond biscotti

250 g/9 oz plain flour, plus extra
for dusting
1 tsp baking powder
pinch of salt
150 g/5½ oz caster sugar
2 eggs, lightly beaten
finely grated rind of 1 orange
100 g/3½ oz whole blanched almonds,
lightly toasted

Preheat the oven to 180°C/350°F/ Gas Mark 4. Lightly dust a large baking sheet with flour. Sift the flour, baking powder and salt into a bowl. Add the sugar, eggs and orange rind and mix to form a dough. Knead in the almonds.

Roll the dough into a ball, cut in half, roll out each portion into a log about 4 cm/1½ inches in diameter and place the logs on the baking sheet. Bake in the preheated oven for 10 minutes. Leave to cool for 5 minutes.

Using a serrated knife, cut the baked dough into 1-cm/½-inch thick diagonal slices. Arrange the slices on ungreased baking sheets and return to the oven for 15 minutes, or until slightly golden. Transfer to a wire rack to cool and harden.

192 Vanilla & almond biscotti

Omit the grated orange rind and add 2 teaspoons of vanilla extract to the mixture with the beaten eggs. Sprinkle 2 tablespoons of chopped blanched almonds on top of the logs before baking and press lightly into the dough.

193 Rosewater biscotti

Omit the orange rind and add 2 teaspoons of rosewater to the mixture with the beaten eggs. Before baking, mix 1 egg white with 1 teaspoon of water. Brush over the dough and sprinkle 1 tablespoon of caster sugar over each log.

194 *Spicy nut biscotti*

50 g/1¾ oz butter, softened, plus extra
for greasing
50 g/1¾ oz caster sugar
50 g/1¾ oz soft light brown sugar
2 large eggs, lightly beaten
275 g/9¾ oz plain flour, plus extra
for dusting

1¼ tsp baking powder
¼ tsp ground cinnamon
¼ tsp grated nutmeg
¼ tsp ground ginger
100 g/3½ oz blanched almonds, chopped

Preheat the oven to 190°C/375°F/ Gas Mark 5. Grease a large baking sheet. Place the butter and sugars in a large bowl and whisk together until pale and creamy. Whisk the eggs into the mixture. Sift in the flour, baking powder, cinnamon, nutmeg and ginger. Add the chopped almonds, reserving 2 tablespoons, and mix together to form a soft dough.

Turn the dough onto a lightly floured work surface and, with floured hands, knead for 2–3 minutes, or until smooth. Divide the dough in half and shape each portion into a log shape measuring about 4 cm/1½ inches in diameter.

Place the logs on the baking sheet and flatten until each is about 2.5 cm/1 inch thick.

Sprinkle the reserved almonds on top of the logs and press into the dough.

Bake in the preheated oven for 20–25 minutes, or until lightly golden brown. Remove from the oven and leave to cool for 15 minutes. Reduce the oven temperature to 160°C/325°F/ Gas Mark 3. Using a serrated knife, cut the baked dough into 1-cm/½-inch thick slices and place, cut-side down, on ungreased baking sheets. Bake for a further 10 minutes. Turn and bake for another 10–15 minutes, or until lightly golden brown and crisp. Transfer to a wire rack to cool and harden.

195 *Cherry & almond biscotti*

50 g/1¾ oz butter, softened, plus extra
for greasing
100 g/3½ oz caster sugar
1 large egg, lightly beaten
200 g/7 oz plain flour, plus extra
for dusting
1¼ tsp baking powder
100 g/3½ oz glacé cherries, cut in half
35 g/1¼ oz blanched almonds,
roughly chopped

Preheat the oven to 190°C/375°F/ Gas Mark 5. Grease a large baking sheet. Place the butter and sugar in a large bowl and whisk together until pale and creamy. Whisk in the egg. Sift the flour and baking powder into the mixture. Add the cherries and chopped almonds and mix together to form a soft dough. Turn the dough onto a lightly floured work surface and, with floured hands, knead for 2–3 minutes, or until smooth. Divide the dough in half and shape each portion into a log shape measuring about 4 cm/1½ inches in diameter. Place the logs on the baking sheet and flatten until each is about 2.5 cm/1 inch thick.

Bake in the preheated oven for 20–25 minutes, or until lightly golden brown. Remove from the oven and leave to cool for 15 minutes. Reduce the oven temperature to 160°C/325°F/Gas Mark 3. Using a serrated knife, cut the baked dough into 1-cm/½-inch thick slices and place, cut-side down, on ungreased baking sheets. Bake for a further 10 minutes. Turn and bake for another 10–15 minutes until crisp. Transfer to a wire rack to cool and harden.

196 *Mixed berry biscotti*

Replace the cherries with 75 g/2¾ oz dried cranberries and 25 g/1 oz dried blueberries.

225 g/8 oz oatmeal, plus extra
for dusting
½ tsp bicarbonate of soda

½ tsp salt
15 g/½ oz unsalted butter, melted
150 ml/5 fl oz warm water

Preheat the oven to 180°C/350°F/Gas Mark 4. Place the oatmeal and bicarbonate of soda into a large bowl and stir in the salt, making a well in the middle. Pour the melted butter and warm water into the oatmeal mixture and mix together to form a soft dough.

Roll the dough out on a work surface lightly dusted with oatmeal. Cut out oatcakes with a cookie cutter. Re-roll any trimmings and cut out more oatcakes. Place the oatcakes on 2 large non-stick baking sheets.

Bake in the preheated oven for 20 minutes, turning them 3 times while cooking. Leave on a wire rack to cool completely.

198 *Cranberry oatcakes*

Add 50 g/1¾ oz chopped dried cranberries to the mixture and knead in before rolling out the dough.

199 *Gingerbread people*   MAKES ABOUT 20

115 g/4 oz butter, plus extra
for greasing
450 g/1 lb plain flour, plus extra
for dusting
2 tsp ground ginger
1 tsp ground mixed spice
2 tsp bicarbonate of soda
100 g/3½ oz golden syrup
115 g/4 oz light muscovado sugar
1 egg, lightly beaten

TO DECORATE
currants
glacé cherries
85 g/3 oz icing sugar
3–4 tsp water

Preheat the oven to 160°C/325°F/Gas Mark 3. Grease 3 large baking sheets. Sift the flour, ginger, mixed spice and bicarbonate of soda into a large bowl. Place the butter, golden syrup and muscovado sugar in a saucepan over a low heat and stir until melted. Pour onto the dry ingredients and add the egg. Mix together to form a dough. The dough will be sticky to start with, but will become firmer as it cools.

Roll out the dough on a floured work surface to about 3 mm/⅛ inch thick and cut out gingerbread people shapes. Place on the baking sheets. Re-knead and re-roll the trimmings and cut out more shapes. Decorate with currants for eyes and pieces of glacé cherry for mouths.

Bake in the preheated oven for 15–20 minutes, or until firm and lightly browned. Leave to cool on the baking sheets for a few minutes, then transfer the cookies to wire racks to cool completely.

Place the icing sugar and water in a small bowl and mix together until it is thick. Place the icing in a small piping bag fitted with a plain nozzle and use to pipe buttons and bows onto the cookies.

200 *Gingerbread ark*

Use animal cookie cutters to make gingerbread animals. Make a Noah's Ark gift box with 2 gingerbread people and several animals.

Index